Loyola Pastoral Series

Formation of Faith

Bernard Cooke, S.J.

Loyola University Press

Chicago 1965

PROGRAM LISTING

First Telecast	1	Faith in the Old Testament
Second Telecast	10	Faith when Christ came
Third Telecast	19	Faith and the development of the individual
Fourth Telecast	27	Faith and its needs
Fifth Telecast	36	Faith and prayer
Sixth Telecast	44	Faith and Scripture: Old Testament
Seventh Telecast	52	Faith and Scripture: New Testament
Eighth Telecast	60	Faith and the Christian home
Ninth Telecast	68	Faith and baptism
Tenth Telecast	75	Faith and penance
Eleventh Telecast	83	Faith and the Eucharist
Twelfth Telecast	91	Faith and the catechist: Introducing the risen Christ
Thirteenth Telecast	99	Faith and the catechist: Sense of community

Imprimi potest Robert G. Humbert, S.J., Vice-Provincial of the Chicago Province, July 22, 1965. *Nihil obstat* John B. Amberg, S.J., Censor deputatus, July 30, 1965. *Imprimatur* Most Reverend Cletus F. O'Donnell, J.C.D., Administrator, Archdiocese of Chicago, July 31, 1965. The *Nihil obstat* and *Imprimatur* are official declarations that a book or pamphlet is free of doctrinal or moral error. No implication is contained therein that those who have granted the *Nihil obstat* and *Imprimatur* agree with the contents, opinions, or statements expressed.

Faith
in the
Old Testament

One of the most important aspects of our human life is that of faith. There are many kinds of faith: faith in the newspapers and their coverage of world events, faith in our friends. But what we are concerned with here is man's faith in God: the faith that is associated with man's life in religion. Without faith and without the ultimate meaning to life, a meaning given by God, human existence has been found to be somewhat frustrating and without purpose.

Unless there is a God in whom we can belive, it is hard to find an ultimate reason for life at all. But we do believe that there is a meaning to life, a meaning which comes from God who not only is, but is interested in us; a good God who provides for us, guiding our life and leading us to our destiny.

But faith is not an easy thing to come by. It is not simple. One of the things that highlights the difficulty of faith is the existence of evil in the world. We have all heard people say: "How can there be a good God when there is so much suffering in the world, when there are people who through no fault of their own are scarcely able to obtain enough food to sustain their physical existence? How can you reconcile this sort of thing with belief in a God who calls himself a Father?"

In how many homes is there sorrow and sickness, disappointment? How many parents watch over with anguish the sickness, perhaps unto death, of their children? They have neither the means to care for them nor the money to provide for doctors. World wars, disasters, human affliction—all of these—point all too clearly to the problem of evil. In the midst of this sort of thing which touches millions of human beings, how can one still say that there is a God who loves us, who is interested in our welfare, and who will provide for us?

And yet if we do not believe in a God, the whole warp and woof of our Western culture has no meaning, because it is predicated upon faith in God. And in our schools, where we educate our children, what purpose would the educational process have if we had no ultimate values, ultimate meanings, to communicate to our students? As we teach them about history and mathematics, about science and literature, we also tell them about the more ultimate things, about the values of human life and the significance of those years of human existence which lie ahead of them. Unless we have a faith to communicate to them, we lack the ultimate dimension of human education. Thus it is extremely important for us to understand what faith really is. By understanding it, we may know how to live it maturely; by understanding it and living it, we may be able to share it with out fellowmen and so give some deeper meaning and significance to their existence also.

In trying to understand what faith really means, it might be well for us to go back to the very origins of what we might call the history of faith. The story of faith, as we know it in the Jewish and Christian tradition, is rooted four thousand years back in that portion of the ancient world called the Near East. There, east of the Mediterranean Sea in the valley between the Tigris and Euphrates Rivers, lies that portion of the world called Mesopotamia. Close to the place where the rivers meet, in the city of Ur, lives a man named Abram. And to Abram, living there in Chaldea, God comes and speaks: "Leave your country, your kinsfolk and your father's house, for the land which I will show you . . . In you shall all the nations of the earth be blessed" (Genesis 12:1-3).

This is what Abram does. Following this God, he leaves his home city of Ur and journeys northward to the city of Haran. From Haran he goes westward to Chanaan. There God again speaks to him and promises that he will make him the father of a great people. This land of Chanaan will be the land of his children and his children's children. Chanaan is a land of great fertility, a place of water in the midst of desert, a place of luxuriant tropical growth, which for ancient people was a sign of wealth undreamed of.

What is the faith of Abraham, as he is called at this moment? The faith of Abraham is essentially a matter of being willing to turn away from the life which he has known and to follow the course of God's direction into this new land. It is to trust in and accept this God who has come to him, describing himself as the Most High God. Abraham now accepts this person, this divine being, this God, as *his* God and promises to worship no other.

In its first stage, then, faith is something quite simple. It is not a complicated saying Yes to many doctrines, not a long list of articles to which Abraham has to subscribe. Very simply it is to follow the call of his God, the God of Abraham, who then also becomes the God of the other patriarchs, the God of Isaac and the God of Jacob. So this, then, is the first stage in what we might call salvation or faith history, the history of those centuries when God was gradually leading his people to faith.

The next stage in our story of faith moves ahead approximately five hundred years. We now come to the land known as Egypt. Here descendants of a portion of those people who had come with Abraham have migrated under the pressure of famine and have settled in an area called the land of Goshen. About thirteen hundred years before Christ, they were persecuted and enslaved by the Egyptians.

As this stage of our faith history begins, there emerges from the Israelite people a man called Moses. Moses is in Madian, on a hillside tending his sheep, when he sees a bush which seems filled with fire and yet is not consumed. From this bush God speaks to him, telling him that he is to lead his people out of Egyptian servitude into a land of freedom.

Moses goes back to his people and tells them about his experiences. Led by Moses, the Israelite people, like Abraham before them, leave the land of Goshen, probably pass through the waters in the area of the Sea of Reeds, and go into the desert. The exact route they follow is not certain. In time they come to a mountain called Mount Sinai. At this mountain the Lord has decided to assemble them and to manifest himself to them in awesome fashion. Fire covers the mountain, a storm comes, and God speaks, telling Moses to tell the people that he wants to forge with them a relationship, a contract, called a covenant. It will be an alliance which will bind God and his people together forever. As a condition of the covenant made at Mount Sinai, Israel is given a law which is a pattern of life for them and which, if followed, will lead them to fulfillment and to peace. The people accept this law at Mount Sinai and make a convenant with their God.

God then leads them up through the desert. They stop for a time and then continue around what we today call the Dead Sea. Finally, he brings them across the Jordan into the promised land. Their journey we call the exodus of Israel out of Egypt.

The journey was an experience of faith, because in making it the Israelites were living their faith acceptance of the God who was Yahweh. He had given them his own name as a sign of familiarity with them; he was the God who would protect and guide them.

As we reflect on this experience, we ask ourselves a second time. What does faith mean? What was the faith of Israel in the exodus? Again we notice that it was essentially the acceptance of a person, this God who called himself Yahweh. But it was not just the personal acceptance of him; they had to accept him on his terms. They had to follow the law that he had given them. This law assured the Israelite people of their own deep, human development and pledged them to serve and worship Yahweh, the one God. Thus we see that faith is already for them now a vision. It is a new way of seeing history and human reality. Many other peoples along the route that Israel followed saw them, but these people did not see Israel's life as being something from God. Only Israel saw this deeper meaning of life, for only Israel was given faith.

We move through the centuries to about the year 1000 B.C. The Israelites are now firmly entrenched in the promised land. We focus on the city of Jerusalem, in the time of King David.

David, as you know, is born near Jerusalem in a little town called Bethlehem. As a warrior he gains great repute and is finally chosen to be the first permanent king of the people of Israel. David unites the whole country and thus realizes the promise given at the time of the exodus. God now comes to David and promises him that he, God, will be with David and with his family forever. God favors this people and their king. As a sign of his favor, there will be upon the throne in Jerusalem a descendant of David forever. Furthermore, in Jerusalem there will stand a temple, built by David's son Solomon, which will be a sign of God's dwelling in their midst. Israel knows that God is not confined by this building. It is, rather, a sign that in some special fashion the God of Israel lives with them and dwells in their midst. This means that all human history begins to be looked upon as a history of faith. It is history seen through the eyes of faith.

At the time of David, there lives, probably in Jerusalem, an author whose name we do not know. We call him simply 'the Yahwist writer," because in writing of the patriarchs he always refers to God as Yahweh. This man writes a magnificent work which scholars today call the Yahwist Epic. It tells the story of Israel from the beginning of mankind in Adam—through Noah, the patriarchs, and the exodus—up to the entrance into the promised land. The Yahwist Epic forms the nucleus, the literary core, the first document around which begin to gather other writings. Out of it emerge the first five books of the Bible, called the Pentateuch.

Notice what has happened at the time of David. Not only is there a clarification of God's promises made in faith to David, but now the faith history of Israel begins to be recorded. We have the first elements of that great document of faith, the Bible. But the kings of Israel, though they start well in David, do not have a history of faithfulness. They are not filled with faith as they should be as the leaders of God's people. They prove to be most unfaithful in many cases, and because of their infidelity the whole northern section of this country breaks away from Jerusalem. There results a divided and oftentimes antagonistic situation among the people of Israel.

But God does not leave his people uncared for. He raises up great men, both in the north and in Jerusalem in the south, to witness to the real meaning of the life of Israel. These are the men whom we call the great prophets. These are men raised up by God with special charismatic gifts. Selected by him to be his spokesmen, they now come to confront the people. They tell Israel that it must begin to live again its early faith. Israel has been the people whom God encountered and led to himself in the desert experience. But Israel has now wandered. She must come once more to understand this God who is the God of the covenant with Moses, and the God of Abraham, and Isaac, and Jacob.

The message of the prophets lays stress on three main elements, which clarify for Israel what its faith is to be. The first element concerns a fact of the present, not essentially something of the past or the future. At the present moment as Amos, Isaia, or Jeremiah speaks, Yahweh is at work in Israel. What is happening is not accidental; God is guiding their history. And if things are going well, it is because God is blessing them. If things are going poorly, it is because God is allowing them to be punished that they may be corrected and come back to him.

The first point, then, is that Yahweh is at work in their midst. The second element of the prophet's message deals with man and with respect for man. Among the Israelites, unfortunately, the poor, the widow, and the afflicted have been forgotten. As a matter of fact, oftentimes they are oppressed by their own leaders, who should be the very ones taking care of them. Man and his greatness are being forgotten. As a result the prophets have to remind man that he is the image of God.

Because he is the image of God, man is free. And because he is free, he has responsibility. Man cannot simply go through life saying that it is too bad that this is what happened. God tells his people, through the prophets, that each man and the people as a whole must encounter God and must face the responsibilities of their own lives. They are free beings made in God's own image.

Third and most important, the prophets speak about Yahweh himself. He is a God of love, a God who cares for them, a God who is faithful to them.

In what does Israel's faith consist at the time of the prophets? It consists in accepting the prophetic teaching: 1) that God is working in their midst, 2) that man is free and responsible and has dignity because he was made to God's image and likeness, and 3) that God wants them to meet and to accept him.

Then comes the time of exile, the destruction of Jerusalem, and a real testing of faith. The people are taken away from Jerusalem, their city, the city of God. No longer can they look upon the temple in Jerusalem as the sign of God's presence in their midst. From their exile in Babylon, they look back toward Jerusalem, knowing that all is in ruin, their temple gone, the city of pile of rubble. Was God faithful? Does faith make sense? Is the man who has believed in God justified in his belief or not? Do they deserve to have God still be their God?

History has answered all these questions. God leads his people back to Jerusalem and sees to it that the temple is rebuilt. By the act of God, answers are given Israel and us. The God of Abraham, Moses, David, and the prophets is a faithful God. He does keep his promises, even though there is nothing we can do to deserve his fidelity.

From the exile Israel learns that we do not deserve to have God be our God. Faith means acceptance of the fact that the God of absolute mercy continues to love us whether we deserve it or not. This is the God we accept. This, against the background of Old Testament happenings, is what faith means.

The faith of God's people in the Old Testament is first and foremost a meeting with God. It is an encounter with Yahweh who gives them his name. He interferes, if you wish; he comes into human history and they meet him there. This meeting with God and accepting him, trusting in his fidelity, is what is required of them in faith. They have to believe that he is a faithful God, and they have to express this by serving him. This service is expressed in worship of him and in fraternal devotedness toward one another. This is the God of the Old Testament of whom the prophets and the psalmist write. Probably no more beautiful word about this God was ever spoken than in the psalm which begins, "The Lord is my shepherd, I shall not want. In verdant pastures he gives me repose; beside restful waters he leads me; he refreshes my soul" (Psalm 22:1-3).

Study outline

Life of faith

Faith gives life meaning
The existence of evil militates against faith in God
Education needs faith for ultimate dimensions

History of faith

Abraham (1850 B.C.)
  God's covenant with Abraham
  The faith of Abraham
    Turning to follow God's direction
    Trust in, and personal acceptance of, God
Moses (1250 B.C.)
  Burning bush, exodus, law, covenant
  The faith of Moses
    Acceptance of Yahweh on his terms
    New way of seeing history
David (1000 B.C.)
  God's fidelity to his people, promise to David, erection of temple
  The beginning of recorded faith history
The great prophets
  Witness to the real meaning of the life of Israel
  Stress three things
    Yahweh at work in their midst
    Respect for the greatness of man, image of God
    Yahweh, a God of love, caring, faithful
  Exile and destruction of Jerusalem
    Was God faithful to Israel?
    Did Israel deserve to have God still be their God?

Nature of faith in the Old Testament

Meeting with God
Trusting in his fidelity
Expressed in worship of God and fraternal devotedness

Study questions

1 "Were one to risk a descriptive definition of the faith that we find described in the Old Testament, one might call it the deliberate and religious orientation of the whole man to God in which man attains authentic existence by acknowledging the saving God as Creator and Lord of history" (*The Bible Today,* Number fifteen [December 1964], p. 967). What points does Father Cooke make about faith in the Old Testament that develops this definition?

2 How does Father Cooke's explanation of faith a) broaden the traditional definition? b) give a deeper relevance to the faith experience?

3 How would you teach the Old Testament (for example, Abraham) to make of it a faith experience rather than a historical study?

Further study

Sacred Scripture: Genesis, Chapters 12-15; Exodus, Chapters 3, 12, 24; 2 Kings 7:8-16, 23:3-6.

Joseph Cahill, S. J. "Faith in the Old Testament," *The Bible Today,* Number fifteen (December 1964), 959-67.

——*What is Faith?* (Doctrinal Pamphlet Series) Glen Rock: Paulist Press, 1962.

Frederick L. Moriarty. "Abraham Our Father," "Moses," "David and the Golden Age," *"Introducing the Old Testament."* Milwaukee: Bruce Publishing Company, 1960. Pp. 1-18, 19-43, 71-88.

Franz X. Arnold. "The Aim of Religious Formation: Faith as the Assent of the Mind and Commitment of the Whole Person," in *Faith and Commitment,* edited by Mark J. Link, S. J. Chicago: Loyola University Press, 1964. Pp. 99-110.

Faith
when
Christ came

The Judaeo-Christian tradition of faith history began to unfold more than four thousand years ago with Abraham. This story can be traced from him to the people of Israel under the leadership of Moses, coming in the mystery of the exodus out of Egypt and into the promised land; then to the kings, David and his descendants; to the prophets; to the decline of Israel and the Babylonian exile; and to the rebuilding of the city. At this point we are on the verge of the great moment in the faith history of mankind, the coming of the Son of God in human form, this man whom we call Jesus of Nazareth.

Centuries of Christians have believed that his coming forms the crisis of the *faith* history of mankind and the crisis of *all* history. And one can trace in the sculpture, the music, the art, and the church architecture of the last two thousand years the story of the faith of these Christians. In buildings based on the Roman basilicas, the early Christians gathered to worship this man who was also God and through him his Father.

Later in the Middle Ages men built those masterpieces of Gothic art, the medieval cathedrals. These spires that soared into the heavens were a witness to the faith of Christians that Jesus was more than just a man; he was God. In every part of the medieval and ancient world, west and east, churches were erected to testify to this faith. Today in the churches that we recognize as distinctly modern, men still gather in community to worship the Father in and through Jesus, his Son.

And as we ponder this history of the last two thousand years, we can ask ourselves what there is about this faith that is so unique. How can Christians really claim to be a community of faith different from so many others? How can they claim that they have the faith among other faiths, one that is unique and one to which men should adhere if they want the full meaning of human life? This is a question that really has to be answered in terms of the appearance in human history of Jesus of Nazareth.

Jesus, a man like you and me, came into Palestine. He lived in the midst of men for a period of about thirty-five years. Born in Bethlehem, living most of his early life in the north at Nazareth, he went as a man of about thirty to the Jordan River in the vicinity of the Dead Sea and Jerusalem. Here John the Baptist opened the public life of Christ by baptizing him. Then, in the north, around the Sea of Galilee, and in Jerusalem itself, he carried on his brief but all-important public ministry.

For three short years he taught and worked miracles. He taught a message of the kingdom of God which was simple and yet very profound: that there is a Father in heaven, his Father and ours, a message which in its simplicity has shattered the whole meaning of human history. His career ended in apparent tragedy, when they put him to death on Calvary, then unexpected triumph, when three days later he rose from the dead.

This is the man whom the early Christians accepted in faith. This is the Jesus of Nazareth who became the object of centuries of Christian belief. As we look at the story of the faith of the early church and ask ourselves what faith meant for those people, we find an answer in the scene of Pentecost if we examine it. On that first occasion of faith, when Peter after the descent of the Holy Spirit spoke to the people, he made clear what Christian faith was to be. What he preached to them was very simple. It was Christ, this man whom they had put to death and who now was risen. What we call the kerygma, the announcing of the message of faith to the early church, is the announcing of the Good News, the fact that death has been overcome, that this man Jesus has risen from the dead, no more to die, and is in his glory so that we may share it with him.

This is the message of faith. This is the nucleus of the creed of all Christianity, the simple but all-embracing mystery of the risen Christ.

Shortly after Pentecost, as the Christians began to gather, the problem arose of instructing them in their faith and telling them what it meant to believe. Once they had listened to the gospel and accepted the fact that Christ was the risen Lord, what did it mean really to have faith in him? How did one go about accepting Christ? The instruction which was given these early Christians is written down as our four Gospels. We can examine it for ourselves to learn what faith is to mean for any of us who are Christians. To delineate more carefully, to describe in greater detail exactly what this faith is, five points can be considered in sequence.

The first of these is that faith demands conversion. This conversion, which is the beginning of faith and its first essential component, is perhaps best exemplified in the Gospels. Of all the Gospel narratives, the ones that teach most clearly the meaning of conversion are the scenes of the vocation of the disciples. Each of the disciples was called in his own way. One was called from the place where he was gathering taxes. The two sons of Zebedee were called from their task of fishing by the seashore, as they were tending their nets and repairing them. A man passed by and said very simply, "Come, follow me" (Mark 1:17). They did. Just as Abraham had had to leave his homeland and come into the unknown, and just as the people had had to leave Egypt and follow Moses into the desert, so also now the disciples were called.

And each Christian is called to leave his past, the context of his previous living, to follow this man Jesus, the Messia and the Lord.

Another important aspect of faith can be seen elsewhere in the Gospels. Perhaps it can best be described as "acknowledged dependence." This dependence obviously is upon Christ and upon his Father. We can understand best what this means by studying the miracle episodes in the Gospels. On many of these occasions when people came to Christ, the thing he demanded of them above all was that they admit their need. When the blind came to be cured or when the disciples were at sea tossed in the storm and in fear for their very lives, they had to turn to Christ and ask him to save them.

This acknowledgment was an opening of themselves to the salvific power of Christ. They had to admit that he was not just a savior in general but *their* Savior; that he could give them sight, health, safety, and life. And Christ did this in faith not simply so that he would be acclaimed. Rather it was necessary for these people that the life of faith might develop in them. The life of faith, as it is described in the Gospels, is a life which is a highly personal reality. It is a life of people; one meant to lead to a personal relationship between ourselves and Christ, between ourselves and God the Father.

Personal relationships cannot be forced on people. No matter how much you like a person, you cannot force your friendship on him. He must be willing to accept it, because friendship is a two-way street. And God, though he be infinite, all powerful, will not force friendship on us unless we are willing to accept him. So when Christ came to translate the mystery of God's love into human form, he did not force his friendship on the people of his day. He wanted to save them; he wanted to give them life. But they had to be open to it; they had to acknowledge their need for him.

The Gospels teach, first of all, that there must be a conversion and, second, an acknowledgment of our dependence upon Christ. This is dependence on a person who claims to love us; and if we really accept him, then faith must demand, third, a trust in the unknown, a real willingness to depend on this person and to believe that he will lead us into what is best for us. We do not know what is coming; nor in a sense did the disciples. But we must trust as they did when Christ had to make clear that he was the one who could save them, that they must listen to him even though they did not know what he was going to endure in Jerusalem—death. They had simply to turn toward him and accept him.

Perhaps the best example of this unquestioning faith was the scene of Christ's prediction that he would give his own body and blood for them. After he had multiplied the loaves, he said to them, "Our fathers ate the manna in the desert . . . my

Father gives you the true bread from heaven" (John 6:31-32). In other words, God had provided for his people in the Old Testament; he was going to provide for them even more in the New Testament. These were mysterious words that they did not understand, and they became more mysterious when Christ insisted, "Unless you eat the flesh of the Son of Man, and drink his blood, you shall not have life in you" (John 6:54). What kind of life was this mysterious thing of which he spoke to them? We know, because we already know the mystery of the Eucharist; but the men to whom Christ spoke then did not know. Faith demanded from them a trust in what was yet to come, in the unknown.

This leads to the fourth element in the faith of the early church, listening. Not only must there be conversion and acknowledgment of dependence, not only must there be trust; but trust must lead to a real listening. This listening is hard for us in any situation. It was hard for Christ's disciples also. In the pages of the Gospels we find that the one time when it was most difficult to listen was when Christ gathered them about himself and began to speak of what made no sense to them at all, that he would go down to Jerusalem and be put to death. He mentioned at the same time that he would rise from the dead, but this was something that they understood even less.

This element of faith is most important in our own experience. As human beings we find it extremely difficult to listen to people. People who are in a conversation can be quite amusing to watch. While someone is speaking, the other people there are all carefully planning what to say next. No one is particularly listening to the individual who is talking. It is a rare conversation in which individuals really open their minds and hearts to accept what someone else is telling them. Yet in the area of faith, it is critically important. Faith must be nourished by the word of God. Only if we listen to what God says to us, only if we listen to him telling us what kind of a God he is, will our faith really grow and develop and become genuine.

It is so easy for us to project our own images onto God, to think of God as having an existence just a little bit greater than our own, instead of as he is in all his infinity. We have to listen to what God tells us in Scripture, in the sacraments of the church, and in the life of the Christian community. For it is in the experience of God working in our midst that we will learn what we are to take in faith.

Just as the disciples found it difficult to accept this strange enigmatic teaching of death and resurrection, so also we Christians will find it difficult to accept what Christ is saying to us, because in essence what he is saying is that we must accept the reality of our own lives and the responsibility of our Christian situation. We must accept the understanding of that situation in terms of the mystery of his own death and resurrection. This is what Christianity says, and it is a difficult saying. When St. Paul was writing to his Corinthian community, he told them that the preaching of this mystery of the death and resurrection of God was a very difficult thing to accept, "to the Jews indeed a stumbling-block and to the Gentiles foolishness" (1 Corinthians 1:23). And it is the same in our day. To the people who do not have faith, Christ's message sounds like foolishness; but for those who believe, Paul tells us, it is "the power of God and the wisdom of God" (1 Corinthians 1:24).

We must listen. This is the fourth aspect of faith which the Gospel pages teach us. There is conversion, acknowledged dependence, trust, listening, and finally identification.

What is this mystery of identification with Christ? It is the culmination of our Christian faith. It is the way we come to the fullness of understanding the mystery of faith. Faith in the early Christian community was quite obviously a matter of accepting Christ. Wherever the Christians went this remained the focal aspect of the mystery: that they took Christ as he described himself, as Lord and Messia, and they lived the mystery of Christ. What is this mystery of Christ which they lived? It is the mystery of his resurrection, not merely saying, "Yes, Christ is risen," but entering into this passover mystery.

To accept Christ means to enter with him into this passover mystery. In baptism we went down into the waters and emerged, as a sign that we accepted the mystery of Christ's dying and rising. More profoundly it was a sign that we really became a part of that mystery. It is not simply poetry or metaphor to say as St. Paul says that we die with Christ, are buried with him in baptism, and then rise with him (Romans 6:4-11). This is a process of accepting a profound identification with Christ. The ultimate mystery of Christian faith is that we really in profound friendship and acceptance become one with this historical individual Jesus of Nazareth.

Nothing in our human experience so profoundly tells us of the meaning of faith as our own experience of deep human friendship. In it we learn the mystery of identification. When two people become friends, each one is willing to be known publicly as the friend of the other person. Not only that, but each is willing to accept an understanding of himself in terms of the other. If someone is my friend, I can trust him enough in love really to accept from him what he says about me. I can trust him enough to listen to what he says I am in his estimation. What is true of our human situation with regard to one another is even truer in regard to our relationship with God. We must listen to what Christ tells us about ourselves. We must accept the identification he gives us because we call ourselves Christian. That is a name which says what our faith is. It is not simply a question of saying Yes to something that has been told us; it is not a question simply of following certain rules and regulations; it is not even essentially a question of performing certain religious actions. What is involved is the acceptance in love of the person Jesus of Nazareth.

These are the principal points to be noticed as we read through the Gospel pages to see what faith in Christ means. Christ lived in the midst of these people, allowed himself to be seen and heard by them, and to be identified with them as a human being. They could accept him into their own human experience, could come to participate in the mystery of his death and resurrection, and his disciples could identify themselves in the actual historical experience for you and me.

In our lifetime also there must be this same conversion, dependence, trust, and listening; but the context of our identification with Christ can no longer be the land and time of Christ. For the people of his own day the context of faith and the acceptance of Christ was to be found in the land of Palestine. Here Christ came and dwelled in the midst of his own. In our day this is not possible. For us this encounter with Christ must come in the context of sacrament.

What is faith when Christ comes on the scene? What is faith as we see it in the New Testament? It is, above all, openness to the mystery of Christ. It is acceptance of this man Jesus of

Nazareth, the Messia and the Lord. It is entry into the mystery of his death and resurrection—and this is in the context of sacrament and the Christian community. It is identification with, total personal acceptance of, and love for this man who is Jesus. This is the story of Christian faith which has progressed through human history for the last two thousand years, even unto our own day.

Study outline

The great moment in faith history is the coming of Christ.
The story of Christian faith is told in the arts and architecture.
Christians claim a community of faith different from all others.

Faith experience of the early Christians

The "man" they accepted in faith
The Good News proclaimed on Pentecost
The Gospels, written instructions defining a life of faith

What faith demanded of the early Christians

Conversion
    The vocation of the disciples
    Call to leave a previous mode of living for a new one
Acknowledged dependence
    The miracles
    Free opening of oneself to the salvific power of Christ
Trust in the unknown
    Promise of the Eucharist
    Trust in the loving care of God for the mysterious life yet to come
Listening
    Understanding Christ's announcement of his death and resurrection was difficult
    Faith must be nourished by what God tells us about himself in Scripture, sacrament, and the life of the Christian community
Identification
    Culmination of Christian faith
    Acceptance of Christ as Lord and Messia
    Entering into the passover mystery of Christ
Life of profound friendship with Christ

Nature of faith

Openness to the mystery of Christ
Acceptance of Christ as Messia and Lord
Entry into the mystery of the death and resurrection of Christ
Identification, in the context of sacrament, with Christ

Study questions

1 How did the faith of the New Testament Christian build upon that of the Old Testament Jew? Was man's faith given a new dimension by the coming of Christ?

2 If we understand the Gospels as "written instruction defining a life of faith," what insights do we receive concerning the miracles, the call of the disciples, the passover mystery?

3 How can teachers provide the conditions for a student's faith encounter with Christ through Scripture, sacraments, and the life of the Christian community?

Further study

Sacred Scripture: Acts 2:22-36; Matthew 9:9, 10:1-42; Mark 1:16-20; Luke 7:1-10; John 6:26-70; Mark 10:32-34; Romans 6:3-11.

Joseph Cahill, S. J. *What Is Faith?* (Doctrinal Pamphlet Series) Glen Rock: Paulist Press, 1962. Pp. 16-24.

P. André Liégé, O. P. "Maturing in Faith," *Bulletin,* January 21, 1962. Grailville: Grail Council of Religious Education.

Jean Mouroux. "Faith a Reality in Christ," *I Believe.* New York: Sheed and Ward, 1959. Pp. 33-37.

Alfonso Nebreda, S. J. "Toward a Living Faith," *Kerygma in Crisis?* Chicago: Loyola University Press, 1965. Pp. 1-20.

Faith and the development of the individual

The story of God's self-revelation to man began with Abraham and continued through the centuries of the Old Testament until Christ. God has been leading us toward himself in belief, even up to the present moment. This is a very attractive reality. But may there not be at the same time a tendency to feel that this faith guidance is also somewhat distant? The key question then arises. What real difference does it make to me whether I have faith or not? Is it impossible for me to become the person I want to be without a faith? Is it so integral to everything that I want to become? Many people think that this is true about faith, and therefore we must face the question honestly. How really pertinent for human life is faith? Three elements to which God himself has pointed in his revelation answer these questions. Faith brings personal fulfillment in terms of maturity, freedom, and happiness. These three things God wants for us, and in terms of these three we will become more profoundly personal. What do maturity, freedom, and happiness mean in themselves? What has faith to say about them? Let us address ourselves to each of these three elements separately.

Maturity is an ideal or reality which we do not grasp easily, something people often talk about, but do not always understand. There are many ways of approaching the concept of maturity, many ways of explaining it. One is to consider three elements of maturity and to see what faith has to say about each of these.

First of all, any genuine maturity demands honesty; second, it demands love; and because of these requirements it demands, third, genuine self-identity. We are familiar with the need for honesty even in the little things of life. But honesty must also be applied to the more critical and basic elements of our existence.

I come back from a fishing trip and tell my friends that the fish which I caught there was honestly *this* large. That is honesty—but a minor form of it. The honesty to which we refer is basic honesty in confronting life, the honesty which permits me to say I am I and not someone else. I am not a great genius who is about to make a world-startling discovery. On the other hand, I am not a person completely devoid of talent either. I am I with the particular gifts that I possess. I am I with my personality. I am I in my particular life situation. A real adult faces himself honestly. He does not pretend to be someone else. He accepts himself for the person he is. This sort of honesty is absolutely fundamental to genuine maturity.

This leads us to the second requirement of maturity, love. Love is something peculiar to human beings. Love is an openness to reality and particularly the reality of other persons. Whereas stones and trees are things that are closed within themselves and cannot reach out to embrace reality, you and I can. Above all, we can turn toward other persons. Love is a growing thing. It starts in earliest childhood when we receive the love of our parents and our friends. For a period we simply take in without being conscious that we must also open out. Then comes adolescence with the experience of learning that love must be a two-way thing. Not only are we to be loved; we must also love. To face that fact honestly is one of the most critical steps in the whole process of growing up and becoming adults. A truly adult person is one who has honestly faced the realities of life, who knows what it means really to live, and who with honesty and love confronts life.

This leads us to the third requirement, self-identity. It flows automatically from the first two. If one has honesty and love, then he can really identify himself as the person that he is, for true self-identity comes with honesty and love. But how does faith fit into the picture? How does it contribute to maturity in terms of the above requirements?

Faith gives a whole new challenge, a whole new dimension, to maturity. Faith, with its message that we are not God—there is only one—and that we are creatures and sons of the Father, makes clear to us that we are what we are. If we believe this, then we cannot really be dishonest. Moreover, in order to come from us, love must be challenged. And the greatest challenge to love that we can have is the love of the infinite God and our fellowmen. These come through faith. If we believe, we have a challenge to our honesty and to our love. In this way we discover our true self-identity. This identity comes in knowing that we are sons or daughters of God the Father, that we belong to this community and are Christian. We discover our worth, because the infinite persons, God the Father, the Son, and the Holy Spirit, love us and are concerned about us. Faith can give a depth of maturity, an openness to life, and an honest grasp of life beyond that of the nonbeliever. In this way faith aids maturity.

The second element of maturity which comes with faith is the element of human freedom. God wants us to be free, and we Americans have a deep appreciation of this. There are other peoples on the face of the earth who enjoy freedom, but I think that this is our heritage in a particular way. As a people we have grown with this ideal, and perhaps because of this God wants the understanding of our freedom to be shared with other peoples of the world and wants this understanding of freedom to flow also into our understanding of faith. Many Americans have an altogether too superficial idea of freedom. It means voting; it means being able to walk down the streets of our cities without being disturbed; it means going where we want in this country of ours. All this is freedom.

But freedom means more: doing what I want to do, leading my life with decisiveness, and setting the course of my own existence and my own development. Yet how many people are excessively swayed and influenced by the things that they see and hear and by the pattern of the life around them. Because they live in a given suburb, they have to dress and entertain the way people do there; they have to have the same kind of houses, the same kind of cars, and so forth. Such people do not have full freedom, because freedom makes two very important demands. To be really free to do and to believe I must love. Love is a liberating thing. If I genuinely love some people, if I have genuine goals in life, then I am freed from many of the false criteria for guiding and molding my life; I am freed from a false quest for popularity. If I genuinely love, I have the security of knowing that I am loved, too, and do not have to depend upon people whose opinions I do not really respect.

Besides being freed in order to love and being freed by love, I must also have a real vision of what life is all about. I must see things as they really are, because only with this kind of vision do I see the various possibilities open to me as a human being. Suppose, for example, that I come home to a dinner of hamburgers. I am not free to choose things other than hamburgers because I see only one thing on the table. But if I see bananas and hamburgers and cookies and ice cream, I have an option because I see more than one thing. If the important choices in life are going to be free, I must have the vision which opens up to the full span of reality. This is where faith comes into the picture. It adds a new dimension to these realities. Faith tells me not only about ordinary human love and how it liberates but also about Christian love, a love which brings a whole new kind of human experience to loving. Christian love is that which Christ has for us; it is our love for him, our love for one another as Christians. When we love this way we are supremely free, and this is what God wants for us. This is precisely why God sent us his own Son and has told us that he is our Father. God the Father so loved the world that he sent his only begotten Son that through him we might live freely and be aware of the fact that we have this love in the full context of the mystery of Christianity. Because of what we know in faith and because of the vision faith gives us of reality, human love is immeasurably deepened in Christianity.

Beyond what we know through science and human understanding, faith gives us a Christian vision of reality. And what is this? By his coming Christ has told us quite simply what life is all about. Before he came men did not know the real meaning of life. Since he has come we know how reality should be seen. A Christian has a vision of the world, human history, and his own situation that a man without the knowledge of Christ and of God the Father could not possibly have. Thus it should not surprise us that Christianity has brought what leads to freedom. It is the whole burden of God's plan of history.

What was God doing for Abraham, the Israelites, David, the prophets? God was freeing them from servitude. One can study the whole of the Old Testament as a story of the liberating power of God and the liberating love of God, and what he started in the Old Testament God has quite obviously fulfilled with the sending of his Son. When Christ came into the world, a man and the Son of God, he came to make us free. He has done this by giving us his own love and his own vision. No one in the world should be more free than we who believe in Christ, who are freed by his vision, freed by his love and that of our fellowman.

The third element which enters into human fulfillment is human happiness. If it was difficult to explain what maturity and what freedom mean, happiness is the most elusive reality of all. We might begin our explanation by considering television commercials. In order to sell things, sponsors invariably appeal to the ideal of happiness.

A classic example might show a group of young people at a picnic—because we think of youth as buoyant and happy. They are apparently having a wonderful time on the beach; all of a sudden everyone's face lights up. You know that something tremendous is going to happen to make them still happier. The latest model of some automobile drives up, and they all run to it enthusiastically. This is the high point of their day. What has the commercial in effect said? An image of happiness has been shown, but one based upon a set of values which imply that happiness comes with material things. Now a certain level of happiness does, but the deepest level of happiness cannot come this way. It comes only when we have the ultimate things that constitute happiness: a genuine sense of security, a genuine sense of belonging, and a genuine hope.

What do we mean by a "sense of security"? Obviously it is not found in a static way of living without danger, problems, activities, or worries. Human beings have to be able to order their lives, to plan, to have some knowledge that the future can be anticipated and be prepared for intelligently. This is the sort of thing we need so that we are not constantly living in fear. We all know what a "sense of belonging" is. We need to have people who mean something to us and to whom we mean something, people to whom we belong, people to whom we can turn, knowing that being with them is coming home. We must have hope and the trust that our life means something, that it is going somewhere, that it is going to have fulfillment, and that in the last analysis it will all make sense. These elements are profound in our human search for happiness.

What does faith have to say about these things? Can faith really do anything about giving us a sense of security? It can. We know that there is a faithful God, and this is the key to his relationship to us. No matter what we have been and what we are now, and even though we have no claim on him, no right to expect his love and his fidelity, God is faithful. He has insisted on that fact. Even when our own family does not give us the acceptance and security we need, even when our health is not good and our future and job insecure, we can still know that there is a being, a person of infinite power and infinite and unquestioned fidelity who has an interest in us. In God the Father, in Christ, and in the Holy Spirit we have a foundation for our security.

Obviously faith gives us a sense of belonging. Why? We belong to Christ! This is what happens when we are baptized. That action is being possessed by Christ as his own. If we accept Christ, he accepts us; and we belong not just to him but to the whole community of people who in the Christian faith share with us this acceptance of Christ. In church and at home we can pray and talk with our fellow Christians, knowing that because we are Christians we have a place where we belong. We can constantly come back to these people with a sense of coming home to them. Faith gives us this.

Faith also confers a third gift. It fosters hope. It not only gives me a deepened sense of security because God is faithful and a sense of belonging with my fellow Christians because I am a Christian; it gives me a whole new basis for hope. This has always been at the very heart of the Christian message. What the apostles preached on Pentecost and during the rest of their apostolate was hope. What they said was that human life now made sense. You can have hope because death has been overcome. Christ himself has overcome it. He has risen from the dead. The Resurrection of Christ is the foundation of our Christian hope—and not just because he died and rose again, but because the risen Lord lives right now. He lives as you and I live, only he lives much more fully. In his risen life, right now, Christ exists not for his own sake; he lives for you and me. This fact is our absolute guarantee that we as human beings will be fulfilled. We will come to completion though we do not know exactly how. We will come to full happiness, full in this life as much as this life can permit and full in the life which lies beyond. We who have faith are meant by God to be the happiest of people. The idea of a believing person's going around with a sad face is completely "out of context." The context of Christianity is one of love; it is one of thanksgiving; it is one of profound, quiet, peaceful happiness.

All of us want to be genuine and complete persons. In order to be such we must achieve personal maturity. Faith helps us achieve maturity because it gives us real understanding of life, honesty, love, and self-identity. Finally, we also need freedom. And again faith comes into the picture. Faith with its vision of life and its love frees us and leads us to true Christian happiness.

Study outline

What real difference does faith make in human life?

Faith gives a new dimension to personal maturity

Elements of maturity
   Honesty, acceptance of self
   Love, openness to the reality of other persons
   Self-identification, result of honesty and love
What faith gives
   A greater clarity to the meaning of self
   The greatest challenge to love
   True self-identity; I am a son of God and a Christian in a community

Faith gives freedom its true dimension

Demands of freedom
   Love, a liberating force
   An authentic vision of reality

Assurance of faith
  In Christ we have a love supremely liberating
  From Christ we have a new vision of the meaning of life

Faith gives genuine happiness

Happiness comes in possessing a genuine sense of
  Security, ordering of one's life
  Belonging, sense of "coming home" to a group of people
  Hope, conviction that life has meaning
True happiness is rooted in faith
  We have security in a concerned, faithful God
  Through baptism we belong to Christ and to the whole Christian
    community
  Death has been overcome in Christ's Resurrection

Study questions

1 What evidence is there that the people of faith in the Old Testament
  and the early Christians experienced greater maturity, freedom, and
  happiness than many of us today?
2 What meaning do you give to these ideas of Father Cooke: true
  self-identity is the result of honesty and love; God is forever freeing
  men from servitude; the risen Lord is our assurance that we will be
  fufilled as human beings?
3 Is it correct to say that the aim of religious education is "man
  fully alive"?
4 How does it happen that for so many young people a life of faith is
  seen as narrow and stultifying?

Further study

Sacred Scripture: John 3:16-21.
Pierre Babin. *Crisis of Faith.* New York: Herder and Herder, 1963.
P. André Liégé, O. P. "Maturing in Faith," *Bulletin,* January 21, 1962.
  Grailville: Grail Council of Religious Education.
——*What is Christian Life?* Englewood Cliffs: Hawthorn Books, 1961.

Faith and its needs

Religious faith, that is to say faith in God, is one of the greatest blessings of human existence. For some four thousand years God has been working in what we call "revelation" to give us human beings religious faith. For human fulfillment faith is required. A person can be mature and happy and free when he does not have an explicit religious faith. But to have the fullness of these things, to be as happy, as free, and as mature as one would like to be and as God wants one to be, a person needs religious faith. Faith gives the insight, the background, the hope, that one needs to find a meaning and a purpose to life. This raises a question for us. If a religious faith is so important in our lives, if we must have it to be in a sense fully men, what do we need to have a genuine faith? What things must there be in order that we believe in God as mature individuals, fully free and happy?

Scripture tells us a great deal about the needs of faith. The first need is one that St. Paul speaks about in his Epistles, a need which the early Christians knew very well. This was the need which we can summarize under the word "preaching."

Unless the gospel of Christ is really preached to men, there cannot truly be any faith response. Unless somehow men hear the word of God, there is no possibility in their lives of opening out and accepting the message of Christ's gospel. Preaching was the first great need of faith in Christ's day as it is in ours. This is the need to which the apostles refer in the Acts of the Apostles as they describe the life of the early church. Preaching is as important today as it was then and will always be so in the life of the church.

What was preaching in those centuries when the early Christian communities began to develop around the Mediterranean basin, starting at Jerusalem and then spreading? The first Christians who gathered at Jerusalem did so because, from Pentecost onwards, Peter and the apostles announced the gospel of Christ. They said that Jesus of Nazareth, like other men, was born, lived, suffered, and died. But unlike other men before him, he did not remain dead. He is risen from the dead and is in our midst. This was the good news the apostles preached; this was the gospel. Men began to accept this truth and to follow the teachings of the apostles, and Christianity began to grow.

Then the apostles left Jerusalem, and the message spread to Damascus, to Antioch, to what is now Turkey and Asia Minor, across Greece, through Italy and Europe, into Africa and eastward, perhaps even in apostolic times as far as India. Preaching was the first task of early Christians, because they realized that faith must begin with a knowledge of Christ's message. Unless the people heard his words, there could be no second step. The apostles were concerned about the millions of men in their day who had not heard the gospel and so lived in hopelessness and darkness, without any meaning to their lives, lived alienated from God. This is why a man like St. Paul needed to be, as he says, "on fire" with the love of Christ and why under travel conditions of the time—not in today's jets and automobiles, but in primitive ships—he went throughout the Mediterranean world to preach the gospel of Christ.

The gospel is not only a need of the past. In our day there are many more millions of people in Africa, Europe, Asia, these United States, and South America. There are many more millions of men than there were in the time of St. Paul who have never heard of Christ and never will. In our day also preaching is the first prerequisite for the existence, growth, and development of faith.

But suppose, now, that we have heard the gospel and that we have found it attractive. We have listened and said, "Yes, I will follow the gospel of Christ." A logical question arises that leads us into faith's second need. How? The answer is we must have instruction.

Instruction can take place in many contexts. We can have instruction in the home, as parents clarify things for children; in informal discussions, conversation situations. We can have it in the pulpit, in the Homily of the Mass; or we can have it sometimes in more formal situations. We can have it in classrooms, whether they be in Catholic schools or in special instruction situations. We can also have it in classes of adults where interested people gather together to have what they believe explicitly clarified. In such classes they are told exactly what has happened in the history of God's dealings with men. The words of Sacred Scripture are explained to them, not simply for the sake of abstract information, but for a more accurate understanding of God.

Faith, genuine faith, is made for reality, not just for words. Genuine faith only grows and develops when it comes into contact with the reality of God; so it is extremely important that our understanding of God, of ourselves, and of our relationship with God be absolutely genuine and true. To put it another way, all of us in our lifetime are in constant need of purifying our faith, to some extent, of elements of superstition; that is to say, of notions directed toward some misinterpretation of God. How many people, for example, worry themselves sick because in their false idea of God they think that he is just waiting for them to make a mistake? For such people religion becomes a burden instead of the liberation that God intended it to be. Tragically inaccurate ideas are in this way conveyed to our children as they grow up. They reach adult life never having really known the God who is, the God who is loving, who wins our friendship and thereby transforms us.

This is the purpose of instruction: to clarify for us precisely what we believe. And it continues throughout our lives.

Our faith started with preaching. Then came the instruction, and this instruction must continue. But we need something further in the development of friendship. Suppose that somebody tells you about a certain John Cline. He tells you what a wonderful person he is, and you listen to everything about him. Maybe this John Cline is a famous person. Perhaps you have read about him and have a rather inadequate understanding of the man; but on that basis alone you cannot form a friendship with him. What is needed? You have to meet him. You have to be able to listen to him talk; and as he communicates, you begin to come to know him. You need this same immediacy of contact with Christ. We must hear him speaking to us in order to have that faith which is friendship.

This leads to the third need of faith. Not only must there be preaching and instruction from without; there must be actual contact with Christ through the word of God in Sacred Scripture. What really is involved here? When I pick up the Bible and begin to read it, I should not read it as I would another book. I find here not simply words about God; this is literally God now speaking to me; this is God's Word.

A situation that makes this fact still clearer is one in which God's Word can be heard audibly, as in a Bible Vigil or Sunday Mass. Here as the priest reads the Word of God to us and explains it in the Homily, his own human words clarify the important word being spoken to us there, the word of Scripture itself. Thus as the lector stands in front of the congregation at Mass and reads the Epistle, he should do so with dignity and clarity. So, too, as the priest reads the Gospel, we should be aware that what is really happening is that Christ is speaking to us through Scripture. These are not merely a human lector's words, not merely a human priest's words; Christ is literally speaking to us through the speakers. These are his words, and on the basis of his speaking to us we can have the immediacy of contact which makes possible a faith that is essentially an acceptance of Christ.

In our day this personal acceptance is possible. This is an experience toward which we are rapidly striving through education—not only in the Mass itself, but also in other activities like Bible Vigils. In them we listen to the Word of God, hear it explained, reflect on it, and then respond. Thus we gradually develop the experience of hearing God's Word spoken to us. Because of our ordinary experience, perhaps this reading of the

Word of God is not so meaningful as it should be, does not have the impact it should have. For this reason, besides God's speaking to us in his Word, there has to be also the speaking that comes in and through the witness of our fellow Christians. This brings us to the fourth need of faith.

After the preaching of the gospel and instruction, even after hearing the word of God in Scripture, we need the witness of Christian lives. We have to discover in our fellowman a "word of God" as it were, which parallels his word in Scripture. Just as the word of Scripture is a "translation" of the reality of Christ which lies behind it, so the life of my fellow Christian is really an expression, a "sacramentalizing," an externalization of the mystery of Christ present in him. As he lives out Christ he is constantly witnessing to Christ's reality.

For many of us the first experience of this kind of Christian witness came when we were children. There at home, gathered around mother as she read to us from books about faith and from Scripture itself, we instinctively and without question accepted what she read as fact. We believed simply because she accepted so naturally the facts that Christ, God the Father, and the Holy Spirit are, that Christ is risen, and that he loves us. We began life with this precious heritage, drawing from the witness of our own Christian homes.

In adult life we encounter other Christians whose witness is as deep, people in whose presence one cannot doubt that God really is. When they speak about Christ or God the Father, or when they go quietly about the business of leading a Catholic life, they do these things so earnestly and naturally that their Christianity cannot be doubted. They do not have to give abstract proofs for the existence of God. They are in a sense a living proof of this reality. This is what is meant by the witness which our faith must encounter in the lives of other people.

But this is still not the final dimension; it is not sufficient to make contact with Christ in the word of Scripture or even in the lives of men. Something more is needed if our friendship is going to grow and develop. We must come into immediate contact with Christ.

After hearing the Word of God and witnessing its effect on the lives of Christians, we must encounter Christ himself. Now this is a key need and a key question of faith, for people logically ask, "If faith is what you have said it is, an acceptance of Christ in love, an encounter with him, how can we meet him?" This is a question that we must face; this is something we cannot turn away from, because this is what Christians from the beginning of Christianity have insisted on. One must actually come into living contact with Christ.

The apostles left Jerusalem to tell others where they could encounter Christ. It is the same place where we today must find our living encounter with him, in the Eucharistic action of the Mass. It is in celebrating the Eucharist, gathering around the altar with Christ in our midst, that we can meet him most profoundly and most intimately. It is there, when we are gathered with him to worship the Father and when his action of sacrifice is our action of sacrifice, that we become one with him. This we celebrate within the action of Communion. We walk up to meet Christ; the priest who is there brings to us Christ under the appearance of food; and we are united with him in the most intimate and profound of human relationships. This is the moment of encounter, and this is the moment of faith. This is precisely when I accept Christ into my person and into my life. This is my act of faith done in the context of the actual experience of Christ, present and working with me.

This is the external side of faith's needs. The word must be announced and clarified. Then each Christian must really encounter Christ, who is here in Scripture, in the lives of Christians, and in the Eucharist. Sadly this ideal does not always correspond exactly with our own experience. Perhaps many of us have heard the passages of Scripture read without realizing God was speaking to us. Perhaps we participated in the Eucharistic celebration on Sunday or on week days without realizing that we were united with Christ in this way. Thus we need to take a closer look at how the Scripture can feed our faith and how we can make the sacramental action, especially the Eucharist, a more meaningful experience in our lives.

There is one further need to which I want to point now. This need is not outside us but within us. Besides the external needs— the preaching, the instruction, the Scripture, and the encounter in sacrament—we need our own openness to God. Unless this final requirement is satisfied, what precedes is meaningless and ineffective. All preaching, witness, and encounter comes to us from God. To receive it, however, we must be open to it. Unless we open ourselves to God speaking to us, his word cannot enter our consciousness or our lives.

One of the things that is unique and so clearly demanding of our openness is the fact that God's word is a word of love. What God says to us is that he is coming to us in friendship. He is offering us his love, and he wants our friendship in return. Love cannot be forced on us. Love is the sort of thing which must be received in order to be given, and it must be received even to be understood. So in this case also, if we are ever to understand the word of love which God is speaking to us in and through Christ, we must open our minds and hearts to it. We must be willing to put aside anything that would contradict love. We must simply, genuinely, and honestly turn to God and say, "Yes, I will listen; I will accept you no matter what you may demand of me."

In the light of this, the scene of the Last Supper where Christ gathered his disciples becomes extremely meaningful in our faith existence. When Christ spoke to his disciples the night before he died, he was speaking to all of us, too.

At that time Christ told his disciples: "No longer do I call you servants . . . but . . . friends" (John 15:15). He also told them that he wanted them to live this word of love: "This is my commandment, that you love one another as I have loved you" (John 15:12). What results from this? "If anyone love me, he will keep my word, and my Father will love him, and we will come to him and make our abode with him" (John 14:23). Through faith God dwells with us.

Study outline

What is needed for a genuine faith?

Preaching

Unless the gospel of Christ is preached, there can be no faith response
The first task of early Christianity was to announce the gospel
Preaching is today the first great need if faith is to come into existence

Instruction

Instruction may occur in the home, discussions, classes, homilies
Instruction is an explicit clarification of what it is we believe

Genuine faith only grows as it comes in contact with the actual reality of God

We have a lifetime need to purify our faith

Reading of Scripture

Scripture is not word about God, but God's Word

When the lector reads, Christ is speaking to us

Faith becomes the acceptance of the person Christ

Witness of Christians

The life of a Christian is a "word of God," an expression of the mystery of Christ present in him

Our faith needs the living proof of those whose faith life is evident

Sacrament

We come into actual living contact with Christ in the Eucharistic action

In a true sense his action of sacrifice is our action of sacrifice

The moment of deepest faith comes in accepting Christ into one's very person and life

Openness

The word of God to us is a word of love, a coming of friendship

The word of God must be received to be understood

Study questions

1 What instances in the Constitution on the Sacred Liturgy show that effort is being made to meet the needs of faith?

2 In what sense is Scripture both sacrament and word? Eucharist?

3 What student-teacher preparation is necessary if instruction is to open the door for a true faith experience?

Further study

Sacred Scripture: 1 Corinthians 1:17-21; John, Chapters 13-15; Psalm 77:1-8.

Gregory Baum, O. S. A. *Word and Sacrament in the Church*. (Doctrinal Pamphlet Series) Glen Rock: Paulist Press, 1963.

The Constitution on the Sacred Liturgy of the Second Vatican Council. With a commentary by Gerard S. Sloyan. Glen Rock: Paulist Press, 1964.

A. G. Martimort and others. *The Liturgy and the Word of God.* Collegeville: Liturgical Press, 1959.

François Taymans d'Eypernon, S.J. "Faith, Man's Communion with God," in *Faith and Commitment,* edited by Mark J. Link, S.J. Chicago: Loyola University Press, 1964, Pp. 111-21.

André Godin, S.J. "Faith and the Psychological Development of Children and Adolescents," in *Faith and Commitment.* Pp. 123-37.

René Latourelle, S.J. "Faith: Personal Encounter with God," *Theology Digest,* Vol. X (Autumn 1962), 233-38.

Jean Mouroux. "Faith a Reality in Christ," *I Believe.* New York: Sheed and Ward, 1959. Pp. 33-37.

Alfonso Nebreda, S. J. "Toward a Living Faith," *Kerygma in Crisis?* Chicago: Loyola University Press, 1965. Pp. 1-20.

George H. Tavard, A.A. *Theology of the Word.* (Doctrinal Pamphlet Series) Glen Rock: Paulist Press, 1963.

Faith
and prayer

A number of the needs of faith are satisfied from outside ourselves: the Word of God, the encounter with Christ in sacrament, the witness of our fellow Christians. All these would be unavailing, however, if we were not open to what God is trying to say to us in calling us to faith and friendship. Let us, therefore, now probe more deeply into the nature of this openness to God, this response, sometimes called prayer.

How is prayer to be used by us in developing our faith? What does it mean to pray? How can we in our lives of prayer grow to intimacy with God? Such intimacy, of course, is vital; faith is not something mechanical. Nor does God impose it on us. Any teacher knows that there is all the difference in the world between simply committing someone's words to memory and genuine learning. What students learn becomes part of them.

If this is so in learning, and it is, then it is preeminently true of faith, because faith involves a personal knowledge. Faith is the acceptance of Christ and an acceptance of the Father. This does not simply mean saying Yes to a formula or an assertion. There must be something else, which perhaps we can put under the name "interiorization." What is told us in faith must really be absorbed. It must become part of our own consciousness and understanding. It must become really a part of each Christian; it is not enough simply to have heard these things. There must be a realization besides. Someone can tell me, for example, in a physics class that fire has the property of burning. I accept that; and if I have to take a test, I can write it down as one of the properties of fire. But if I put my hand too close to fire, I will experience this property personally, realizing it myself. So it must be with faith.

But before realization must come reflection. That is to say, I must ask myself when I hear about the truths of faith: "What does this mean? How do I know this is true? What difference does it make to me as a person?" Only by engaging in such consideration will I pass beyond mere hearing and superficial knowing to deep reflection. In the area of faith, however, another element is needed for interiorizing, that of acceptance. Ordinarily I must be willing to learn in order to learn. In the area of faith this is particularly true, for I am dealing here with a person, Christ. And if I am really to open up and reflect upon what he should mean to me, I must be willing to accept the implications of Christ in my own life. If I am not willing to face up to who Christ is and who the Father and the Holy Spirit are, to confront these truths, I will not really reflect carefully. I will not realize all that Christ means, because the implications would be too great for me to accept willingly.

Thus if I am to have real interiorizing, I must begin by accepting; I must then reflect upon what faith tells me Christ is. Only then can the realization of what Christ is become part of me. This is what we mean by prayer. In prayer I must be willing to listen carefully to what God is saying to me in Scripture, in sacrament, in the life of the Christian community. I must in my prayer turn and listen, reflect and then respond, and realize that this is what prayer is meant to be. There is another way of approaching prayer that may be easier to understand because it is closer to human experience. That is by considering ordinary friendship. Prayer is meant to be something that simple, not something complicated. It ought to be the establishment of a friendship between ourselves on the one hand, Christ, the Father, and the Holy Spirit, on the other. If we take a good look at what friendship is and then apply it to Christ, we will understand in a simple but very profound way what prayer involves.

What happens when I form a friendship with another human being? Examine any close relationship. How did it grow? Obviously, one thing required was association. One cannot form a friendship at a distance. It can begin that way, as happens with people who are "pen pals." They start by writing, but even that writing is a form of association. If a friendship is to flourish and develop in depth, friends must meet constantly. Being together is not enough, however. There must also be communication. There need not be many words. As a matter of fact, as the friendship develops there will not be much chattering; the talk will be more serious, more simple, more profound. There must be a real communicating with my friend, a constant associating with him in order really to become bound to him in friendship.

The same thing is true of Christ. Because Christ came in human form, we human beings can associate with him. We can communicate as human being to human being and thus form a friendship with this person who is as human as we are but who is also the Son of God. This is what prayer is meant to be, simple direct converse with God.

There is a difference, however, in that Christ has already spoken to me. My prayer is always by way of response to him. He has spoken to me already in Sacred Scripture. He speaks to me every time I participate in sacramental action, particularly in the action of the Eucharist. He speaks to me in the activities of my life and the Christians who surround me. All these are his side of the process of communication. My prayers are meant to be a genuine simple response to him. That is why true Christian prayer should not be purely a recitation.

Please do not misunderstand me. There is a place for the recitation of set prayers, but we must be careful that these recited prayers really express what is within us. There must be a real interiorizing of these formulated prayers, so that they do not become a mere verbalizing, a simple external expression with nothing on the inside. Such would be foreign to a real development of a friendship in any human situation. It also applies to our relationship with Christ. You wouldn't talk to your human friend by reciting a formal memorized speech. Your friend would look at you and wonder whether you were sick. That is not the way we talk with friends. So prayer should be a very simple direct response to Christ as he is, as he has revealed himself.

There is another aspect to friendship, however, to consider. If someone is really my friend, I am willing to let that person be who he is. Being someone's friend involves genuine acceptance on his part and on my own. I must let this person really be himself; and I must be willing to be myself. If someone is my friend, I do not tell him, "Well, now, I don't like you; I want you to be so and so instead of being yourself." This would be the end of the friendship. So also with respect to God. Honesty and acceptance of the concrete reality are important. If I am to have Christ as my friend, I must let Christ be as he is; and I must be who I am. A friendship involves not just communication, not just association, but the final dimension of genuine, honest acceptance of both persons.

When people pray, they often tend to put on a mask. Watch people as they go into a church. So often on the outside they are happy, joyous, joking, at ease. Then they go into what they apparently consider a somewhat artificial situation. They put on their prayer face; they become solemn and unlike themselves, instead of just being natural, just being who they are. Christ knows who we are. He wants us to be ourselves.

There are also certain things that must become part of our consciousness if prayer is to be genuine. The first of these is the fact—and notice that it is a fact—that Christ is. Both of these words are really important: that it is *Christ* and that he *is*. Let us start with the verb. It is not what I would like Christ *to be* that is important when I pray, but the awareness, the consciousness, that he truly *is* now.

I must also be conscious of who this person is. He is Christ risen, and it is not up to me to decide how. He really is the risen Lord, and because he is risen he is triumphant. So when I turn to him, I do not think of him as sorrowful or sad or worried. He is none of these things. He cannot be. As the risen Christ he is in his glory. When I go to him, therefore, it should be with a certain sense of wonder and happiness, rejoicing with him because he is in this situation of triumph. Above all, I should realize that he is not only the risen, triumphant Lord but a Lord who is alive. He is living a life such as you and I do not yet enjoy.

Christ in his risen state has a vibrancy, a vitality such as you and I do not understand yet—and will not understand until we begin to share in the fullness of Christ's risen life. It is important to know that Christ is alive if we are to pray simply and genuinely in response to him.

The same thing is true about God the Father. I must know that the *Father is.* Again, both words are important. The Father really *is.* *Father* is important, because it is not left to me to imagine what kind of person he is. He is a very definite person, and he has told me who he is: first and foremost, of course, the father of Christ. He is not fatherhood in general, not fatherhood "pushed" to the infinite degree. He is a person, the father of another person, Christ. Just as I can turn to a certain man and say "This is George's father" to identify him, so I can say of God, "This is the father of Christ."

But he is also our Father. He is not simply fatherly toward us. You and I stand in a relationship of sons and daughters to the Father. When we come to him and call him Father, we are doing something very profound in the area of faith, are we not? Faith is an acceptance of the fatherhood of God and our own sonship. Do we not express this when we pray? We should turn to him realizing that he is Father and accept him as such in a simple but important act of faith.

Talking about who Christ is and who God the Father is leads almost inevitably to the third necessary element in our consciousness: I must accept the fact that *I* am. Here, of course, we need not concentrate so much on the *am.* What is important is the *I.* It would seem rather obvious that I am not somebody else, but we know that in our associations with people, even in our association with God, even in our dealings with ourselves, we often do not want to acknowledge who we really are. I do not want to admit that I am really I. Sometimes I like to pretend that I am someone else, but I am not. I am this person, and it is a great part of maturity and human wisdom really to acknowledge myself. This is the next thing which prayer requires.

If there is the acknowledgment of self, prayer is, as it should be, very natural. Praying to God should in a way be the most natural thing in our lives. Many of us were fortunate in that we grew up in family situations where prayer was taken for granted. Perhaps as we grew older, we lost some of that simplicity, that naturalness. If so, we should regain it, knowing that God wants us to be ourselves. Being ourselves is required for honesty in prayer. Honesty requires that I acknowledge not only myself but also that I am related to Christ. This is important if I am to understand what it means to be a Christian, to stand in a most important relation to Christ. These, then, are the three things which we must realize and make our own, if we are really to have a simple, genuine, deep, active prayer life.

Another element of the development of a friendship, and therefore of prayer, is rather mysterious. It is something all of us take for granted because we live with it all the time, something that perhaps we do not reflect on as deeply as we might.

This is the whole aspect of presence. What do we mean by presence? How does the idea of it touch upon prayer? Presence can be viewed in a very superficial way. One can think of presence as simply "being there." For example, at the moment, you may be in the presence of some pieces of furniture. But the presence of a speaker or writer is quite different because he affects your consciousness. This latter is the kind of presence which must come into our prayer, the realization of our deep personal relationship to Christ—not only that he is but that he is ours. This sort of relationship should become an atmosphere in which we live so that little by little our lives are permeated with the awareness of Christ's presence. I do not have to pretend about his presence; I do not have to invite it; I do not have to invent it. He is. Logically, therefore, the answer to the question often asked, "Where can I pray?" is "Anyplace." One need not be in a church, chapel, or some specially consecrated spot to pray. Wherever I am Christ is, because I am a Christian. In a quiet, simple, direct way, prayer can be a continuous thing in my life. I can and should pray, aware of the fact that God the Father, the Holy Spirit, and Christ are wherever I am.

Prayer is most essentially a growth in deep acquaintance with Christ, through Christ with the Father, and in union with this other person who is the Holy Spirit. Obviously, if this growth is to develop, our relationship to these persons will have to be constant. If I turn to God just once a month, there will not be much development of acquaintance with him. Even if I go to him once a week, at church on Sunday, our relationship is not going to deepen and develop into a simple, natural association. What is required is something more constant. It need not be highly formalized. I ought to pray naturally.

Private prayer is not the most important area of Christian life, however. All genuine Christian prayer is meant in the ultimate analysis to lead to participation in the Eucharistic action of the Mass. Thus it is when we gather around the altar—brothers and sisters in the deepest sense, in union with Christ—that we are most deeply Christian. Here, united to Christ most profoundly, we say together with Christ and in union with the Holy Spirit, "Our Father who art in heaven."

Study outline

Encounter cannot lead to faith except with the response of openness called prayer

Requirements of prayer

God's word must be interiorized
    Religious knowledge is often superficial, notional
    Realization comes through reflection
Faith demands acceptance for realization

Prayer as friendship

Association, a recurrent pattern of meeting
Communication, a conversation, not merely saying prayers
    Christ has communicated
    Prayer is a response
Acceptance
    Let Christ be who he is
        Christ *is* risen, triumphant, vibrant
        Christ is who loves us
    Let the Father be who he is
        The Father *is* here and now
        He is *Father,* ours and Christ's, and we celebrate this fact in the Eucharist
    Accept the fact that I am who I am
        Honestly
        Simply
        Naturally
Presence
    Christ is constantly and profoundly present
        We can pray wherever we are
        The mystery of Christ's presence is the atmosphere of Christian living

Prayer must be a regular experience climaxed in the Eucharistic action

Our relationship to Christ is most truly expressed in the Our Father
In union with others
Gathered around his altar
United with Christ in the Eucharistic action

Study questions

1 What are student difficulties in prayer? Do they find prayer to be a "friendship situation"?
2 What is the role of prayer in religious education? What forms of prayer (group meditation, psalms, prayer-song, and so on) should be used in a religion class?
3 What can be done to make liturgical and formal prayer more meaningful?
4 What is the role of formal prayer in the school community?

Further study

Sacred Scripture: Psalm 62; Matthew 6:5-15; 7:7-11; Mark 1:35; Luke 6:12, 11:1-13, 22:42; Acts 2:42.

Leonard Boase, S. J. *The Prayer of Faith*. St. Louis: B. Herder Book Company, 1963.

Louis Evely. *That Man Is You*. Westminster: Newman Press, 1964.

Richard Gräf, C.S.Sp. *The Power of Prayer*. Westminster: Newman Press, 1961.

Romano Guardini. *Prayer in Practice*. New York: Pantheon Books, 1957.

Charles Moeller. "Initiation to Prayer and Liturgy," in *Teaching the Sacraments and Morality,* edited by Mark J. Link, S.J. Chicago: Loyola University Press, 1965. Pp. 159-62.

Michel Quoist. *Prayers*. New York: Sheed and Ward, 1963.

James C. Turro. *Prayer*. (Doctorinal Pamphlet Series). Glen Rock: Paulist Press, 1962.

Faith and Scripture: Old Testament

It is rather critical in the development of our faith that we come into intelligent, adult contact with the Word of God, because it is meant to make our faith more accurate and more deeply personal and to deepen our sense of conviction that these things which we believe are true. What does the Old Testament say to our faith? This is not to ask simply what it says in itself, but what it says that is meaningful to me as a believer. Another way of asking the same question is in terms of the need for forming and developing faith. Does the Old Testament help in this development? If so, how?

There has been a most important development in Scripture studies in recent years, a development that some people fear because they think that what these Scripture scholars are doing might destroy or hurt our faith, or perhaps destroy the validity of the Bible. Actually, just the opposite is true. The real professionals among the Scripture scholars are in no way destroying our faith; they are clarifying for us what the Bible really says, so that when we believe, we are directing our attention to what God is saying to us in the Old Testament.

One of the things we have to remember in order to understand the Old Testament is that one cannot read it intelligently by isolating its passages. One must see the progress, the development, of Sacred Scripture. We must remember that God has dealt progressively with his people, from Abraham's time forward. These centuries of God's intervention in history form the whole progress of the faith development of Israel as a people. Israel's is not just ordinary history; it is a sacred history; it is the history of the faith of a people.

What is God trying to communicate through this account? We can distinguish two kinds of knowledge; about himself, our God, and about ourselves. These are the two "poles of reality" about which the Old Testament revolves. It tells us profoundly who we are, but it does that by describing ever more clearly and sharply and deeply who this God is by whom we are directed, saved, and delivered.

What does the Old Testament tell us about God? The first thing it tells us is that he is a God who saves, and not in some abstract way but in the concrete facts of history. God wants to give us life and freedom; when he finds us in servitude, our lives threatened by chaos and evil, he gives us freedom and life. But because chaos must be overcome, he also gives us order.

Knowing what these three gifts of God are helps us see the whole sequence of man's history in a clear light. We can first look back to the creation of the world, which may not pertain, strictly speaking, to sacred history, except in that the people of Israel interpret this as such. The next stage is the call of Abraham. What God did for Abraham tells us what he wants to do for us. He took him out of the land of the Chaldeans, where he lived in obscurity and idolatry (and very likely in a certain amount of servitude and even enslavement), and God called him to a land of his own. Why? Simply so that he would have land? No, it was because owning land represented having freedom. He could have dignity. He could be a full person. This is what God was doing for Abraham; he was leading him into a situation in which he could fully realize himself as a man, where in dignity he could be the father of a great new people. What God wanted from this man was that he accept freedom and life in faith. We can learn from this that our God is a freeing God, a liberating God, a life-giving God.

The next stage of Old Testament history and its development was the exodus. About 1300 B.C. a group of God's people left Egypt, where they were slaves, crossed the waters into the desert, and stopped at Mount Sinai. There God gave them the covenant and the law. What was God doing? What was he saying in his great deeds? He was liberating, was he not? He was freeing his people who had been enslaved. He was destroying the threat to their lives. The pharaoh was apparently trying to wipe out these people by killing all the male children so that it would be impossible for them to continue as a distinct group.

God entered into battle with the pharaoh and overcame him. As a result the Hebrews were free to pass over into the promised land. They now had a life of their own, a life which could be guaranteed by security and by peace, guaranteed not only by the fact that God had freed them, but also because he had given them a law. The law put order into their existence. They became a community. Without it, the life of the people would have remained chaotic and disordered; they would have ceased to exist as a people and would have vanished quickly from the pages of history. But they did not, because beginning with Sinai this law guided and ordered their lives. It was itself a principle of life and freedom. Just as he led Abraham, the God of Israel led his people to freedom and life in the exodus.

Then about 1000 B.C. King David came upon the scene. He was Israel's first great king, founder of the Davidic dynasty. As David entered adulthood, the very life of Israel was being threatened. A mighty warlike people, the Philistines, had come in from the Mediterranean area and threatened to wipe out the people of God. God raised up David as a leader, and within a comparatively short time he drove out the Philistines. As the king of Israel, he established the unity of the entire people. They could again live in peace and security in their own land. He established Jerusalem as the political and religious capital and thereby brought order to both religious and civic life. Through this great man God raised the people to a higher level of freedom, responsibility, and life.

Not all the kings were like David. As a matter of fact, many of them were unfaithful. A rather tragic period of Israel's history came when the people were led into exile in Babylon. There they faced a profound religious crisis. God had been revealing in this whole process that he was still a faithful God. Now his people wondered whether he was still the God of Israel or if he had abandoned them after pretending to be their God. God raised up a great prophet in exile, Ezechiel, who promised that Israel would live again. God caused him to see the famous vision of the dry bones. Ezechiel was led out in spirit and was shown a great valley covered with dried-out bones of men. God asked, "Shall these bones live?" And Ezechiel answered, "I know not, Lord." Then God showed him the bones coming together to form skeletons. Then tissue, sinew, and muscle covered the bone. Finally, his spirit breathed over all, and living men once more stood there. A full army had been revived.

God was saying that he would bring Israel back to life. And this is what happened. The people were freed from exile and returned to Jerusalem, where they rebuilt their city and its temple as a pledge that their God was faithful. He had not abandoned them. He would always lead them back toward life and fullness of life in freedom and order.

This process has been repeated through the ages, through the mystery of Christ, and into the still-existing mystery of the church. The God of the Old Testament is a life-giving, saving, and personally concerned God. He does not direct the world by remote control, looking down on men as pawns, as pieces of a puzzle. He is personally concerned about Israel as a community and about each individual Israelite. He is pointing this out in the actions which he performs for his people. He also points it out in the writings of Israel's prophets and, above all, in the symbolic speech of their prophetic oracles. There are many symbolic images, such as the vine. Israel is a vine, and God the vine dresser. He planted his people, a vine, in the promised land, developed, and cared for them as any careful vine dresser would tend his own vines. The history of Israel follows a pattern of God's planting and tending a vine.

But the vine is not a fruitful one. The prophets, therefore, speak sadly about this. Speaking in all probability at the gate of the temple as the people pass by, Isaia calls out: "My friend [God] had a vineyard on a fertile hillside [Jerusalem]; he spaded it, cleared it of stones, and planted the choicest vines; within it he built a watchtower, and hewed out a wine press. Then he looked for the crop of grapes, but what it yielded was wild grapes" (Isaia 5:1-2). Israel is this vine which has not been faithful to God and has yielded only wild and sour grapes.

Another image which many of the prophets used is that of the shepherd, an image drawn from the life of the people. The Israelites were from the earliest days sheepherders; they knew what it meant to care for animals unable to provide for themselves, and they knew that they had to watch out for them. God now used this figure to speak about his people to tell them that, though they were in exile in Babylon, he was their shepherd. Ezechiel speaks of this clearly in referring to Israel's exile and her kings' failure. The shepherds who should have provided for the flocks had not done so, and God says: "I myself will look after and tend my sheep. As a shepherd tends his flock when he finds himself among his scattered sheep, so will I tend my sheep. I will rescue them from every place where they were scattered when it was cloudy and dark. I will lead them out from among the peoples and gather them from the foreign lands; I will bring them back to their own country and pasture them upon the mountains of Israel" (Ezechiel 34:11-13). This is a picture of God leading his people back from exile to their homeland, where they may pasture forever in peace. You can recognize in this passage the background for those beautiful parables in which Christ describes himself as being the Good Shepherd who goes out to take care of his sheep.

A third symbolic image in the writings of the prophets takes us into a more personal area. This is the image of God as father. There are several places in the Old Testament where God is spoken of in this way. We take these for granted, because we have become accustomed to the fact that God is our father. It was a great revelation to the Israelites that God should see his relationship to them as that of father to children. In the eleventh chapter of the prophecy of Osee, God says: "When Israel was a child I loved him, out of Egypt I called my son" (Osee 11:1). Notice how God speaks of the people as being his son whom he has called out of Egyptian bondage.

The final image to be noted is the most profound of all. It is the one in which God through the prophets speaks of himself as being the bridegroom or the husband of Israel. Israel as a people is the bride, the wife, of God. But she has been unfaithful, and God time and time again has had to chastise Israel, trying to convince her of his love for her. In the second chapter of the prophecy of Osee is found the tender, and yet disappointed, language of God. God first says that he will reject Israel. He has had enough of her, chasing off with these false gods and abandoning him, and he has written a bill of divorce. He will not even acknowledge her children as being his. Yet in the second half of the chapter God repents, and says that he will go to claim her. He will find her with her lovers and will call her back to himself, make her his bride again. It is a beautiful passage: "So I will allure her; I will lead her into the desert and speak to her heart . . . She shall respond there as in the days of her youth, when she came up from the land of Egypt. On that day, says the Lord, She shall call me 'My husband,' and never again 'My baal.' Then will I remove from her mouth the names of the Baals, so that they shall no longer be invoked"; to Israel he says: "I will espouse you to me forever: I will espouse you in right and in justice, in love and in mercy" (Osee 2:16-22). The prophet thus speaks of Israel as the bride of God and of God as the bridegroom, the husband, of his people.

Two aspects of God draw our attention. God is a life-giving, freeing God; and he is, second, a highly personal and concerned God. The life of faith does not only speak to us about God; it is also meant to speak to us human beings about what it means to be a man. Conclusions should be drawn from this revelation of God. What God has been insisting on from the very beginning of his workings with Abraham, the Israelites in the exodus, David, the prophets (and to the present time, as a matter of fact) is that he wants us to be free. And if he has freed us, obviously he wants us to live as free men, not to be driven by every whim, not to yield in sheer conformity to some pattern of life. He wants *us* to live our lives, and because we are free and have the power of decision, he wants *us* to decide. He wants us to be men of responsibility, to take the world and make it ours. As Abraham had to make his world, and Moses his, and David the world of his day; so you and I today are meant to make our world and to be responsible for it. We are told early in the Old Testament that God planted a garden [the world] into which he put man to take care of it. This is what God does for us. In the course of sacred history he has been pointing out to his people—both to those in the Old Testament and to us who read it as our heritage and as revelation—that we are to take our world into our own two hands and to be responsible for it.

But in order that our world develop and that we live, we must be careful that the forces of chaos do not overcome us. We must listen to the Word of God, the Word of his law and the living Word, Christ. This is what the Old Testament speaks of, particularly in the beautiful passage in Isaia in which God's Word in Scripture is called "an everlasting imperishable sign" (Isaia 55:13). Isaia says: "Just as from the heavens the rain and snow come down and . . . watered the earth, making it fertile and fruitful, giving seed to him who sows and bread to him who eats, so shall my word be that goes forth from my mouth; it shall not return to me void, but shall do my will, achieving the end for which I sent it" (Isaia 55:10-11): the freedom and the life of man.

Study outline

What does the Old Testament say to our faith?

How is the believer to regard the Old Testament?

He is to make intelligent, adult contact with the Word of God
He is to seek scholarly clarification
He is to consider Scripture the history of the faith of a people

How is God revealed in the Old Testament?

He is a God who saves; he wants to give us life, freedom, and order
    Abraham; God called him to a land of his own, a sign of freedom and dignity
    Exodus; God saved his people from death, made a covenant, and gave them the law which ordered the life of the community
    David; through him God drove out the Philistines, established Jerusalem as the center of the life of his people
    Exile; God is a faithful God; Israel shall live again (Ezechiel 37:1-14)
He is a personally concerned God
    Vinedresser (Isaia 5)
    Shepherd (Ezechiel 34)
    Father (Osee 11:1)
    Bridegroom (Osee 2)

How is the true believer revealed in the Old Testament?

He is to be free
He is to be responsible for shaping his world
Growth in faith needs the life-giving Word of God (Isaia 55:9-11)

Study questions

1 How do you interpret Father Cooke's sentence, "What he did in the Old Testament God wants to do for us"? How is this sentence completed in Bishop Henri Jenny's statement, "The liturgy is the Bible still in progress"?

2 If teaching history involves teaching meanings, interpretations, trends, how does such teaching differ from that of the Old Testament?

3 In *The Bible Today* (February 1965, p. 1027), Father Eugene Maly urges all teachers to be positive, not negative, in their approach to Scripture. What is the difference between the two approaches? What is the difference in the effect on the students?

Further study

Sacred Scripture: Ezechiel 37:1-14; Isaia 5; Ezechiel 34; Osee 2; Isaia 55:9-11.

Louis Bouyer. *The Meaning of Sacred Scripture*. Notre Dame: University of Notre Dame Press, 1958.

Celestin Charlier. *The Christian Approach to the Bible*. Westminster: Newman Press, 1958.

Lawrence Dannemiller, S.S. *Reading the Word of God*. Baltimore: Helicon Press, 1960.

Albert Gelin. *The Key Concepts of the Old Testament*. New York: Paulist Press, 1963.

Jacques Guillet. *Themes of the Bible*. Notre Dame: Fides Publishers, 1961.

Frederick Moriarty. *Introducing the Old Testament*. Milwaukee: Bruce, 1960.

Kathryn Sullivan, R.S.C.J. *God's Word and Work*. Collegeville: Liturgical Press, 1958.

Carroll Stuhlmueller. *The Prophets and the Word of God*. Notre Dame: Fides Publishers, 1964.

Bruce Vawter, C.M. *The Conscience of Israel*. New York: Sheed and Ward, 1961.

Faith and Scripture: New Testament

What does the New Testament say to our faith? How is the reading and the hearing of the New Testament meant to be part of the formation of our Christian faith? These two questions raise two others, the most important that human beings can ever ask. The first deals with the very heart of the New Testament: Who is this man Jesus of Nazareth whom we call Christ? Is he just another man, a great man but purely man, or is he somehow more than man? Is he really, as the early Christians and many since believed, the Son of God? This question is inseparably linked with the second: What does it mean to be a Christian? What is a Christian? We use this name to refer to ourselves, do we not? What do we really mean by it? Unless we know with some clarity and depth the answer to these two questions—Who is Jesus? What does it mean to be a Christian?—we cannot go very far in the development of a mature faith.

We are not the first ones to ask these questions. They were aksed by the earliest generations of Christians in Jerusalem. From Pentecost onward these early Christians gathered together in small groups which gradually grew into larger ones, particularly on Sunday, the first day of the week. They would congregate for the celebration of the Lord's Supper, the Breaking of the Bread, the Eucharistic action. They would come together for the meal, and at the beginning the one who was presiding (generally an apostle at that time) would break the bread, speak over it the words that Jesus had used at the Last Supper, and distribute it. Then they would have the meal, at the end of which they would take the cup of wine, bless it with the Eucharistic words of Christ, and give it to all.

In all probability, during the meal or perhaps for a time before or a time after, they would converse with one another, particularly the new Christians who had recently come into the church, asking the apostles: "What does all this mean? We know that this Jesus was here and that he died and rose, but what else did he do? What was he like? What did he talk about? What are we supposed to be as Christians?" During these gatherings there developed the apostolic catechesis, that is to say the preaching, teaching, clarification, which came from the apostles as they met with these early Christians. From this catechesis our Gospels developed. As the apostles taught, people gathered together these teachings. Then, as they moved to other places— there were not apostles everywhere—the apostles began to be put to death as witnesses to Christ. The early Christians decided to write down these recollections, this historical explanation of the apostles. It is in this recorded catechesis that the collection of books called the New Testament finds its origin.

What does this New Testament literature tell us? Many more things than we will ever be able to understand in the course of our entire lifetime. Basically there are two realities, Christ and ourselves, revealed in it. To simplify matters we can divide the New Testament into three large sections in order to consider the teaching contained in each.

The first of these sections is the book of the New Testament called the Acts of the Apostles. This book is just exactly what the title says: a simple historical narrative of the experiences of the early church, beginning with Pentecost and ending two decades later. It describes the way the early Christians lived; but more importantly it tells us how the apostles preached, what their message was, how they catechized. Always they tell us about the man Jesus. This is important. When the apostles began to preach at Pentecost, they did not preach doctrines; what they talked about was a person, Jesus. What they said about him was simple but very important: he is risen from the dead. Because he is risen, he is the Messia, the fulfillment of all that Israel had anticipated. He is more; he is the Lord. That is to say, he is really God. So the early church, from the beginning of the apostolic preaching, gave to Jesus, because he is risen, the titles Messia and Lord.

The Acts of the Apostles tells us again and again that the apostles preached this way. It also tells us something about the early Christians, and therefore about us because we also are Christians. We must never forget that when we read the Acts of the Apostles, we are reading what pertains to our faith. What does the book of the Acts of the Apostles tell us about the early Christians? It tells us that they were sent by Christ and the Holy Spirit to do essentially two things: they were to announce the Gospel of Christ as Christ himself had commanded; they were to preach the gospel to every creature, to the ends of the world, telling men that Jesus is risen, that he is Messia, and that he is Lord. This knowledge is still crucial for human beings who must answer the question "Who is Jesus of Nazareth?"

Second, the Christians were sent to all parts of the world in order to celebrate the Eucharist. In celebrating it, the Christians proclaimed Christ, and Christ was in their midst. The Risen Lord was there as they reenacted the continuing mystery of his death and resurrection.

The Acts of the Apostles contains the earliest expression of the faith of the first Christians, the faith which we share. Out of the Christian assemblies of these early decades came the recorded teaching of the apostles, which took slightly different forms in different portions of the ancient world. Though there is just one gospel (and really we should not speak of it in the plural form, for there is only one gospel of Christ) still that gospel is seen from four different points of view. Essentially, however, all four writers say the same thing: they tell us about Christ. They tell us about ourselves, but emphasize Christ. The reason is that, if we are going to understand what it means to follow Christ, what it means to be like him, then we have to know what he was like. The Gospels tell us that he was truly man, as you and I are; that he was born, grew, developed, came into adulthood, was hungry and thirsty, slept, suffered, died, and then passed into new life. He was fully and integrally man, but he was not just another man; he was that man who was sent from the Father for our sakes. He was the man whom the Father sent to tell us about the Father. He came because the Father loves us. He came to announce that fact to us. He was sent from the Father to redeem us.

The Jews comprised the large part of the Christian society. Christ had come for them, so it was very important to point the fact out to them. But it is also important for *us* that this man is the Messia of Israel, the fulfillment of all Israel's hopes, the perfect Israelite, the perfect Son of Israel. The Gospels detail the various aspects of the Messia: the fact that he is the Davidic King whose coming was prophesied, the fact that he fulfills the wisdom of Solomon, the fact that he is the Servant predicted in the Old Testament. Each of those facets of his role is considered and "deepened," until we discover that Christ is not just man but a Divine Person. He is in the fullest sense the Son of God. This is the incredible message of the Gospels. This is the almost unbelievable answer to the question of who Jesus is. He is all of these, but most profoundly he is the Son of God, come to transform man and the whole of human living, so that human history and our lives here and the meaning of our lives will never again be the same. God became one of us.

The Gospels tell us about ourselves also. With the coming of Christ, a new concept of wisdom is given us. It is not an abstract or esoteric type of wisdom, but a wisdom which is very simple and yet very profound. The deepest answers to human life are given us, not in a law, a code of behavior that we have to follow, but in a man whom we follow as a friend and an ideal. This new way of life is really Christ. If we want to live the way he taught, live as he lived, see the world as he saw it and still sees it, love what he loves, and have his set of values and balanced view of human life, then we must live as he did, in honesty, in straightforward acceptance of life, and above all in open, generous love of our fellowmen and of God the Father.

In the Gospels' simple and beautiful message a new way of life opens before us, because the Son of God has come into our midst as a true man to teach us what it means to be truly a man.

The Epistles make up the third large section of the New Testament literature. Whereas the Gospels spoke almost entirely about Christ, and about ourselves only in terms of him, the Epistles spend a great deal of time telling the early Christians about themselves. This is reasonable since most of the Epistles (particularly the great Epistles of St. Paul) were letters written to Christian communities. Paul is advising them about everyday affairs of living as a Christian community. He reminds them of the things he has already taught them and deals with the concrete problems that they face. He deepens their understanding of what it means to be Christians in community. For us, also, he clarifies the Christian identity, not just individually but as a community, so that we will understand our responsibility.

The Epistles tell us first who Christ is. Those to the Ephesians and the Colossians are most profound. They say that Christ is a Divine Person and that he is also man.

When the Epistles discuss the Christian community, we notice an interesting growth or deepening of understanding. The early Christians were conscious of being a community. That is to say, they had gathered together largely because they accepted one Lord, the risen Christ, and because the Holy Spirit was in their midst. They wanted to celebrate the Eucharist as a community, but their structural understanding of themselves was somewhat limited. They did not pay much attention to it at first, but gradually they became aware of their distinctive identity as a religious group which stood apart from Old Testament Judaism. The different Christian communities around the Mediterranean basin could be called churches, but they were also *one* church. They were, in a sense, one community of faith.

We can tell from St. Paul's Epistles that as he wrote to the different churches, these Christian communities became aware that they really formed one community of faith, one church. Soon their perception increased. This can be seen in St. Paul's Epistle to the Corinthians, and above all in the letter to the Ephesians, where he spoke of the Christian community, ourselves, as being the body of Christ.

People are sometimes very vague in their thinking with regard to this concept. Jesus, who is Christ because he is risen, still exists as man; and he is present in the midst of Christians, to give us life continuously.

My life is directed by my head, which controls all my actions, so that when I gesture, speak, or move, the life direction travels from the head to the rest of the body. So also, somewhat analogously, Jesus lives still in our midst, communicating life to us as our head. We do something for hims in return. As the visible human body reveals the physical and spiritual presence of a person, the Christian community indicates Christ's presence in the world. People who see Christians know that Christ is the risen Lord and that he still abides in our midst. We are the sign of Christ's presence; and we are, in a sense, his hands and his voice. In our actions, in our gesture, in our words, people should be able to discover the presence of Christ.

This dictates the way we Christians are expected to live if we are to be the people in whom the world can discover Christ. We must live lives of faith and charity. The Epistles primarily counsel us to show forth Christ, our head; the Acts of the Apostles tells us about our Christian predecessors; the Gospels show us Christ.

But while we can read in the New Testament about Christ and about ourselves to inform our faith, the name "Scripture" is given to both the Old and New Testaments, the Word of God. The term means more than that the Bible was inspired by God. Scripture, both Old and New Testaments, is the living Word of God. That is to say, it still lives as word, and when we read Scripture we are literally hearing God speak. When in the Eucharistic situation at Mass on Sunday we hear the Epistle and the Gospel read to us, it is the word of God being proclaimed to us. While it is a human being who is speaking—the lector who reads the Epistle or the priest who reads the Gospel—Christ is speaking through him. We have gradually to accustom ourselves to an awareness that Christ speaks to us in these readings. We should listen to them intensely and carefully, as we do when a close friend has something important to say. The most important thing we have ever heard is what Christ has to say: I want to tell you about myself and what I intend to do for you to make you a happier person.

We would listen very carefully to a friend, would we not? This is the experience that we as a community must learn to have when we read or listen to the Bible in our churches, particularly in the Sunday celebration of the Eucharist. There, as we listen to the Gospel and Epistle, we must know that Christ himself speaks to us. We must open our ears, minds, and hearts to listen to that word—not just because it is polite to listen when somebody is speaking, but that we may have life. The word which is being given is the source of the life of faith. Unless we listen to this word, faith cannot be formed.

Faith is the acceptance of a person. We can only accept him as he tells us about himself. This Christ does when he speaks to us in Sacred Scripture.

Study outline

What does the New Testament say to our faith?

How is the New Testament meant to form our Christian faith?

Adult faith rests on two important questions
    Who is Jesus of Nazareth, the Christ?
    What does it mean to be a Christian?
The Gospels developed from apostolic catechesis
    At the Sunday gatherings for the Lord's Supper the apostles clarified the meaning of the event
    These recollections of the historical explanations were recorded

New Testament literature puts us in contact with the teaching of the apostles about Christ and about ourselves

The Acts of the Apostles, simple historical narrative of life in the early Church which tells us how and what the apostles taught
    They taught not doctrines but a Person: the Risen Christ, the Messia, the Lord
    The early Christians were sent by Christ, by the Spirit
        To announce Christ, the Gospel
        To celebrate the Eucharist, Christ present
The Gospels; one gospel from four points of view
    Primary emphasis was on Christ
        Truly man
        A man sent by the Father to announce the Father's love, to redeem us
        The Messia, the perfect Israelite, king, prophet, servant
        Son of God come to transform human life
    The new way of life is Christ
The Epistles
    These letters deepen our understanding of the Christian community
        Early Christian consciousness of being a community
        Distinctive identity as a religious group
        Awareness that all Christian communities form one church

The one church is the body of Christ
Jesus exists in our midst and gives us life
We are the sign revealing Christ

The word of God in the Old and New Testament is a living word

God speaks to us now, particularly at the celebration of the Eurcharist
The Word is the source of our life of faith

Study questions

1 Why is it so important for the Christian to understand the historical development and the use of literary form in the New Testament?
2 The Gospels are testimonies of faith, rather than biographies of Christ. How do we share with students, rather than "teach" the Gospels?
3 Christ speaks to us in the Gospels, acts with us in the liturgy, and lives with us in the Christian community. Relate these ideas to the religion class.

Further study

Barnabas M. Ahern, C.P. *New Horizons.* Notre Dame: Fides Publishers, 1963.
François Amiot. *The Key Concepts of St. Paul.* New York: Herder and Herder, 1962.
Georges Auzou. *The Word of God.* St. Louis: B. Herder Book Company, 1960.
Joseph Bonsirven, S.J. *Theology of the New Testament.* Westminster: Newman Press, 1963.
Lucien Cerfaux. *The Church in the Theology of St. Paul.* New York: Herder and Herder, 1959.
Roderick A. F. MacKenzie, S.J. *Introduction to the New Testament.* New Testament Reading Guide 1. Collegeville: Liturgical Press, 1960.
Quentin Quesnell, S.J. *This Good News.* Milwaukee: Bruce Publishing Company, 1964.
Thomas Sheridan, S.J. *The Church in the New Testament.* (Doctrinal Pamphlet Series) Glen Rock: Paulist Press, 1962.
David M. Stanley, S.J. "New Understanding of the Gospels," in *The Bible in Current Catholic Thought,* edited by John L. McKenzie, S.J. New York: Herder and Herder, 1962.

Faith and the Christian home

The home is the first context in which faith is formed. A Christian when he is baptized receives essentially the power of faith. Yet our baptism in infancy did not give us the full consciousness of faith, an operative faith life, but only the power to grow in this direction. The home is really the cradle of faith, for here active living faith comes into existence. It is in the home that we receive those first glimmerings of consciousness. We pass from having only sensation and a gradually dawning awareness of the world around us to a higher plane of perception.

Psychologists tell us how vastly important are the early formative years. Psychological impressions made upon us in the first moments, weeks, and years of our life remain with us in one form or another throughout all time. Our first choices and decisions to open out to others are primitive inclinations to allow ourselves to be received by them, to insist on being made the center of attention. On the other hand, we sometimes tend to shut ourselves off and retire. This whole dawning life of human personal consciousness which takes place in the home is of critical importance for the human person.

Since faith is the transformation of our life of consciousness and love, this power of faith should also be maturing during these years. It is in the home where faith first awakens. The child comes to know what it means to believe and to discover those persons—Father, Son, and Holy Spirit—in whom he believes. He learns what it means to be a Christian. The impressions about Christianity which he acquires in these years are of utmost importance. So also the choices he begins to make with regard to God and living as a Christian are choices which will have an impact on the whole development of his faith life.

If the home environment is so important, what precisely is the function of the parents in these years? Exactly what is it that they are meant to do for their children? First, the parents are to function in a situation of witness. This means more than merely talking about Christianity or giving explicit instruction in the various aspects of Christ, Christianity, and the Christian life. Witnessing is a matter of directing one's whole person, by everything that one is and says. It is pointing to the reality of Christianity, to the fact of its verity. It is not enough to tell children about Christ. Young people coming into adulthood "know the answers." They have been catechized, told about Christianity. But is it real to them? Is Christianity a matter of fact? Parents must convey Christianity to their children, not by simply telling what it is, but by living it out in their daily lives. When the parents talk about Christ, they must talk about him as of someone real. They must talk about God the Father as of someone who really exists. They must not talk about Christ as of some historical personage but as of someone who lives now. This is extremely important in the life of a child. It is in the reflected faith of the parents themselves that the child slowly comes to see this as fact. There is Christ; there is God the Father; there is the Holy Spirit; there is the church; and there is God's love for me.

Besides these, the parents must also point to the pertinence of Christianity. A child may hear occasionally that he is a Catholic. He may hear the name of Christ used now and then by his parents—and let us hope not in some profanity. He may hear God the Father referred to. But if these occasions are rare, if such matters seem of little importance in the life of his parents—who are primarily occupied with their work, recreation, new cars, furniture, entertaining, television, movies, and so on—if the constant stream of attention and conversation and interest is on the material, what impression does the child almost inevitably gain? He sees faith as something relatively unimportant, since it scarcely seems to matter in the lives of the two persons who for the moment are very largely his world. Parents, by their own lives and what they say and how they live, must reflect the reality of Christianity and its pertinence to their own lives.

They must also point to a third thing: the attractiveness of Christianity. The reason this is so important is that faith involves choice. It is the acceptance of Christ on his own terms. We are inclined to accept what is attractive to us. If we do not want something, we do not choose it. So if Christianity is not attractive, and therefore important, to the child, he will not concern himself with it as an adult either. As he is attracted by other things, he is likely to forget all about his life of faith.

Thus the attitudes and the remarks of the parents during the formative years are of critical importance. It is in the context of the home, the day-by-day awareness in the lives of those who surround him—his brothers and sisters, yes; but above all these two key adults—that he finds his own values, his own view of the world, his own dawning consciousness of their insight in the light of what they think important. If parents do not witness to the fact of the importance and the attractiveness of Christianity, the child (unless something unusual happens later on in life) will be seriously deprived with regard to the growth of his faith life.

Now let us suppose that the parents in question have given this kind of witness. Then a second great area of need presents itself. Instruction must be given in the faith. It must be formed so that when the child growing into adulthood accepts Christianity, he does so with accuracy. There must take place in the home a whole process of instructing the child. Two points should have primacy. The instruction of a person in the faith should not be concerned primarily with doctrines or practices. It is essentially instruction with regard to the persons of Christ and the Father, because faith is an acceptance of these persons.

As a child begins his life of conscious faith, this faith must be directed toward Christ as he is. Children should be told how

Christ was, but what is more important is how Christ is now and who God the Father is now. The child must learn who these persons are and that they love him and are concerned about him. Parents must be very careful not to turn God the Father into a bogey man, to help themselves in keeping law and order in the home. Too often parents whose child misbehaves, perhaps because he is not well enough trained, try to solve the problem by bringing God in as a sanction—as if God will punish children for being poorly trained. The result is that the child grows up, not with an attitude of love and trust, but of fear. What should be in his heart are love for and trust in these two persons.

But there is more that must be told the child as his faith develops. Christianity is living in community. One does not become a Christian only as an individual; one belongs to the family of God. And what better context is there for explaining how Christianity is a family than the family situation in which the child is growing? But the explanation of Christianity as a community and that of the persons of Christ and the Father should always be done prayerfully. Children pray very easily. They see prayer as a very normal and natural thing. When you tell them about God's being present, they should be encouraged to talk to God in an easy fashion.

Two allied attitudes also have to be developed in the child's faith life: Christian responsibility and a sense of moral values. This is not just a matter of giving the child *dos* and *don'ts,* a list of sins. It is something more fundamental. It is teaching him the basic fact that he must face the results of his own actions; he must take responsibility for what he does and for the persons who are his world. If he hurts them deliberately, he is responsible for having hurt them, and it is up to him to try to help them over the harm he has caused. That is why moral attitudes should be developed essentially in terms of love. Has he given love to those to whom he should give love? To his parents? To his brothers and sister? To his playmates? Or has he in any way denied love to them? If he begins to accept his responsibility to develop these attitudes in the home, he gradually comes to discover his identity as a Christian, and this is what a parent must teach him. What does it mean to be a Christian? What does it mean that he was baptized? What difference has this sacrament made in his life?

That, of course, leads right into the subject of the gradual preparation of the child for full participation in the Eucharistic act. It is true that some instruction can take place in the parish or school, but the real conditioning, the orientation for an active, though simple, child participation in the Eucharist must come in the home.

Finally and basically, the child must learn acceptance of the concrete situation of his life. He must learn to accept himself as a Christian, the responsibilities which are his, and his identification in terms of Christ and the Father. If he learns to accept this kind of identification, then he will be truly Christian as he is meant to be. These are realities that the home must communicate to children if their faith is to be a clear and integral assent to Christianity as it really is. This is the more or less explicit type of catechizing. It need not be very formal nor follow a question-and-answer format, unless the child is naturally of an inquisitive nature. The parent then can answer questions raised.

Another area of the home and its impact on faith is much subtler and yet extremely important. Everything we understand about life we see somehow in terms of our own experience. Inevitably we project something of ourselves and what we have been and what we have known into all the new situations we encounter. We understand a definition of *hearing* because we hear. When somebody talks about sight, we follow his train of thought because we know what it is to see. And when faith comes into our life, it deals with the most fundamental of human experiences. If the child, growing from early life into adulthood, does not have an integral experience of life in the family situation, he does not have the full foundation upon which faith can grow.

For example, a child's relationship with his father can be happy or in some cases disastrous. It can be a situation which lays a foundation for peace and happiness in the years that follow, or it can create lasting psychological problems. What is the father supposed to exemplify? What is the father the "sacrament" of? What is he supposed to suggest to his children in the experience of the family? He should represent, first of all, loving authority. Inevitably in the home he will be some sort of authority figure: either a good one or a bad one. And because he is so naturally going to exemplify authority, the child as he goes out of the home and into adult life is going to carry with him the judgment of authority which came out of that situation. If as a child he could associate authority with love, if the authority in the home was loving, the child will be helpfully integrated in all the situations of authority he will encounter for the rest of his life: in school, in government, in public life, in religion. But if he has reacted against authority, if in the home authority is something exercised in harshness—perhaps even with vindictiveness—then fear and rejection are necessarily associated with anything which speaks of authority. How does a person like that react when you tell him that God is a father? Fear, distrust, and antagonism inevitably arise in the emotional life of the person. You can see, therefore, how vital it is to have a father who exercises authority with love.

Closely connected to this, of course, is the whole notion of law. Many people rebel against law in any form, because the association of law at home with father was an unhappy one. How can you tell those people that God has given law to us so that we will be free and happy? All law means to them is confinement and restriction.

Finally, the early father-child relationship is meant to provide the foundation for trust and security. We need as children and as adults some absolute upon which we can rest; something on which we can ground our own frailty, our own insecurity. If experience with a father has not given that in early years, a very deep insecurity and lack of trust in life can often, and generally does, result. And how can you tell a person who has not learned to trust in his father to associate security with father? How can you tell him to believe that God the Father is the source of all his trust in himself and in life?

Similar to this is the more basic need for love. The family context is an important teacher in this regard. Our faith tells us that God is love; but for one to understand that, he has to have some understanding of what love is. What happens to the child who grows up in a home where there is no love between father and mother, where there is wrangling, bitterness, and even hatred? This child often cannot even believe that there is a thing called love. When you tell him that God is love, he does not know what you are talking about. One of the most priceless treasures parents can give their children is their love for one another. If children grow in this atmosphere, if they develop in it, if they are almost "bathed" in the warmth and love of their home, they can grow into integrated human beings. They are able to be fulfilled by the love of God. Of course, parents' love must also be extended to the children; and it will be if they genuinely love one another. If children are the recipients of love, it is possible for them not only to respond to love, but for them to understand and give it. Without this sort of atmosphere, this implicit teaching with regard to the most basic things of faith, faith has great difficulty in developing any vitality in the person's early years. And if it does not begin to live then, it is almost a miracle of grace if it begins to live at all.

How parents witness to their faith, instruct their children, and give them love and security in the home is of critical importance in the formation of faith. Parents might well reflect upon one way to apply themselves to the words of Christ at the Last Supper: "By this will all men know that you are my disciples, if you have love for one another" (John 13:35). Can this not apply to the home? Is it not exactly the way in which children are meant to discover that their parents are Christians, real followers of Christ, that they have love for one another? Children seeing love exhibited will know what Christianity is: the acceptance in faith of the mystery of God, who is love.

Study outline

Faith in the Christian home

The home is the first context in which faith is formed

Baptism does not give an operative faith but the power to grow in faith
Early impressions and first choices are of critical importance in the development of the human being
Since faith is the transformation of the life of consciousness and love, the power of faith should mature from earliest childhood

What is the function of parents in the early life of children?

A parent is a witness
  He points with his whole person to the reality of Christianity
  He reflects the pertinence of Christianity to human life
  He reveals the attractiveness of Christianity
Parents must carefully instruct the child
  Instruction is more concerned with the Persons of the Blessed Trinity than with doctrines

Christianity is a matter of living in community, the family of God
The explanation should be given prayerfully
Parents must help the child develop responsibility and moral values
These should be developed through the child's understanding of love
His family experiences prepare a child to participate in the Eucharist
The child must learn acceptance of himself as a Christian
Faith builds on the fundamental experiences of his home life
Relationship with father
Fatherhood is the "sacrament" of loving authority
Law is related to freedom and happiness
The foundation of trust and security is necessary for faith
Experience of love
The experience of love is needed to understand that God is love
The atmosphere of love permits children to understand love and
respond to it
One of the priceless treasures parents can give their children is their
love of one another

Study questions

1 If the school is an extension of the home, which requirements for the formation of faith in the home pertain to the faculty and the atmosphere of the school?
2 How can parents and teachers effectively nourish a living faith and at the same time respect the freedom of a young person?
3 What are the differences between the faith of a child and that of an adolescent? What human experiences underlie each?
4 How can parents and teachers help each other in working with the Holy Spirit to form Christians?

Further study

Clayton C. Barbeau. *The Head of the Family*. Chicago: Henry Regnery Company, 1961.

André Godin, S.J. "Faith and the Psychological Development of Children and Adolescents," in *Faith and Commitment,* edited by Mark J. Link, S.J. Chicago: Loyola University Press, 1964. Pp. 123-37.

——, editor. *From Religious Experience to a Religious Attitude.* Chicago: Loyola University Press, 1965.

Jean Mouroux. *From Baptism to the Act of Faith.* Rockleigh: Allyn and Bacon, 1964.

Marc Oraison. *Love or Constraint?* New York: P. J. Kenedy and Sons, 1959.

Klemens Tilmann. "Initiation to Life with God," in *Faith and Commitment.* Pp. 169-84.

Faith and baptism

Establishing the identity of a child or adolescent as a Christian is vital to his growth in faith. It is important, therefore, to explain to a child what baptism is, what it has done for him, and how it fits into his life of faith.

We know that from the very beginning of the church, even in the early centuries, the connection between baptism and faith was very clearly seen. Baptism was looked upon as being essentially a profession of faith by the new Christian. Even today, as a candidate for baptism enters the church, he is asked, "What is it that you seek?" The reply is faith. Not only does baptism begin our life of faith; it sets the pattern for Christian living. It directs us toward a certain way of life, a certain way of thinking, a certain way of being: the Christian way. To understand our Christianity, we have to understand what took place the day we were baptized.

Baptism first introduces us into a community or, if you will, into a family. Shortly after a child is born into a family he is baptized. We sometimes forget that by his baptism the family context is broadened. Not only does he now belong to the family into which he was born as a human being, but he is brought into God's family, the Christian community.

One was more aware of this truth in the days when most Christians were baptized at the Easter Vigil. Then, the people would be gathered together to see those to be baptized brought into the church. The literal entering into and being received by the community made it very apparent that a member was coming into the church. Even though the symbolism is not so obvious in the way we baptize today (generally taking place on a Sunday afternoon with comparatively few people present), still the intrinsic action of the sacrament is one of introducing the new Christian into the family of God.

One of the things that really stressed the family aspect of Christianity for many centuries was the fact that the parents sponsored the child. Nowadays two other individuals are usually the sponsors. Perhaps some day we shall go back to the old practice. There is a great significance in having the two people responsible for this child's human birth bring him for new birth into the full family of God.

In this whole notion of being introduced into the community there is a deeper dimension. The community into which we are introduced is called the church, the body of Christ. It is not just another grouping of people, not just a massing together of those who believe in Christ. This community of faith is really a living organic unit. The living Christ, the risen Lord, is still in our midst in this community; and we are a family unit because of our faith acceptance of him. The church is really the living community of those who accept Christ in faith as risen and alive today. Each one of us is introduced to, made a member of, this body at baptism. Christ touches us and makes us his own. Through baptism we are in a real, profound sense, possessed by the risen Christ who dwells with us. His presence makes the community of Christians his body. If we say that the first thing that happens in baptism is that we are introduced into the Christian community, we must understand in the full sense that we are brought through baptism into the mystery of Christ. In being made a member of his body, we are profoundly bound to Christ himself. Christ has taken possession of us in baptism.

This means that he allows us to join him now in carrying on his mission in the world. It is a twofold mission: of acknowledging and worshiping his Father, and of going out into the world of men to unite them with himself for a fuller life, to lead men through himself to the heavenly Father. This mission Christ gave to his disciples. At one point he told them, "As the Father has sent me, I also send you" (John 20:22). And in the last visible appearance to them, just before the mystery of his ascension, his words to his disciples were "Go, therefore, and make disciples of all nations, baptizing them in the name of the Father, and of the Son, and of the Holy Spirit" (Matthew 28:19). We who belong to the Christian community share this mission of Christ.

When we join any organization, any society, any group, we share its aims and objectives. When we become part of this community of faith we are given the church's aim, its objectives, the aim and objectives that Christ himself gave it when he made it a missionary community. The church of which we are members *is* essentially a missionary church. It is impossible to be a Christian—joined with Christ, a member of this community of faith—and not to have a missionary orientation. In baptism not only do we join a community; we are already commissioned. The Christian is sent forth for two purposes, worship and apostolate.

To see only the externals of the sacrament is to miss the more profound dimension of what took place in our baptism. Christ put his mark on us. He touched us, "branded" us as Christians. The mark we bear is not visible, but by it we are directed to a share in Christ's own priestly act. What we call the "sacramental character" leads us to share Christ's own mission. This has a twofold aspect to it, just as Christ's mission does. Sharing in his priesthood involves being directed toward apostolate and worship. Baptism, in a sense, ordained us to celebrate the Eucharistic sacrifice. The reason we can is that we bear the character and power of Christ's priesthood, his commission to acknowledge his father.

But we do not just remain at the altar, though this is the focus of priestly power. The mission of Christ has a second aspect. We are sent from the altar into the world of men. We are sent to transform, not just individuals, but the very patterns of human society. As we receive the vision of Christ in the action of the Mass, as we learn from him the message of his transforming love, as we understand that he wants us to be free people, we must carry that message into the world. In this way the second phase of our priestly activity as Christians is accomplished, so that the lives of men are gradually changed by the vision, the charity, and the great mystery of the freedom of Christ.

Besides our introduction into the Christian community and the priestly orientation which we call the sacramental character of baptism, there is a third aspect to our Christianity. Through the sacrament we receive a new identity. We become sons of God. Ever since our initiation into the Christian life we have heard of this fact in a rather "neutral" way. We must see that the one to whom we are related now is God the Father. As Christ, who in his own baptism in the Jordan heard the voice of the Father saying to him, "This is my beloved Son" (Matthew 3:17), so we in our baptism are acknowledged as sons of God. We are directed toward him. The wonder of the situation is that God becomes our father. This association is no vague one. The idea that if we are Christians, somehow we have an indistinct relationship to the "Divine Something" is not correct. God the Father is really *my* father. I personally am related to him by baptism. Because of this, a transformation takes place in me. I am changed. The very center of my being is transformed, a necessary prerequisite to sonship. If I am to open myself to God the Father, then I must have the capacity to do so. As a human being I do not. This is why a transformation is required, the transformation we call "grace."

The mystery of grace really involves a whole new kind of living. It is the opening of my person, the expansion of myself, which enables me to reach out and touch the Divine Persons. The fathers of the church talked about this way of life as being more than an elevation of my way of living, rather a "divinization." A man is born once into human life. With baptism comes a new birth and it deserves to be called just that. It is a new dimension of living, literally a divine dimension, which makes it possible for me to be receptive to the mystery of the Divine Persons—to become part of their family situation, if you will. I can now approach the three Persons as they really are: God the Father as father, Christ as his son, and the Holy Spirit as the Holy Spirit. I now possess a new depth of personality because I am transformed into a son of God.

A fourth aspect of baptism has many practical ramifications. Baptism is essentially an orientation to the mystery of the Eucharistic action of the Mass. This has been known since the time of the baptism of Christ in the Jordan. When Christ heard the Father speak to him, he was already promising to enter into that new covenant at the Last Supper. So also in our baptism we made promises: the promise to renounce Satan and all his works, and the more fundamental promise of participating in that new covenant situation, the Eucharistic action.

Have you noticed that in some of the new churches the baptismal font stands right at the door of the church? A person entering must pass the font where he himself became a Christian. What does this say to him? When he was baptized he pledged himself to fulfillment, to go further into the church—not just into the church building but into the whole mystery of the church's life. This is why he was baptized: to participate in the continuing mystery of Christ's death and resurrection. Passing the baptismal font should remind him of this.

In the earliest days of the church the baptismal fonts were sunken pools into which steps led. The candidate would enter the water-filled pool and emerge to signify his first participation in the mystery of Christ's death and resurrection. Each partaking of the Eucharist was a deeper entry into this mystery.

The first conception of baptism involved entering the church building and being ceremonially exorcised and anointed. The candidate was then brought to the baptismal font into which he descended as a sign of death. Water in itself signifies a dying, does it not? Water can destroy. If I stay under too long, I shall drown. Water carries this meaning. But in baptism it represents not just dying but the death of Christ. The symbolic association of the candidate with Christ in death was more readily apparent then than today. Christ remained in the tomb for three days—there is the mystery of Christ's burial—and so the Christian not only goes down into the water, but is immersed for an instant, symbolizing burial. Then he comes out of the water to signify resurrection, because water is also a source of life, not just any kind of life, but the risen life of Christ.

You can see what baptism said for the early Christians. They were really aware of the deep meaning of the mystery of death, burial, and resurrection. In baptism they entered into this mystery for the first time. But they went beyond that into fulfillment in the Eucharist. This was apparent in the Christian "rites of intiation." The ceremony involved baptism, confirmation, and the Eucharist. After baptism the bishop would anoint the Christian on the forehead and crown with the chrism, the special ointment which is still used in confirmation. Then they would advance farther into the church. The third stage was a celebration of the Eucharistic action. A Christian was not totally initiated into the mystery of Christ until he had participated in this, shared in the Body and the Blood of Christ, celebrated Christ's death and resurrection in Eucharistic sacrifice.

That was the initiation. For the early Christians, baptism was something which led right into the whole mystery of Christian living. It should do so for us, too. We should try to see as clearly as they that our baptism is essentially a family affair. We are brought by our own family to the church and introduced into a larger family, the people of God. As members of that community we share in its commission to worship the Father and to go out into the world as apostles. We share in the priesthood of Christ. Like the early Christians, we are sons of God. The Father transformed our lives to make it possible to live the life of faith. We are directed toward the fulfillment of our baptism in the celebration of the Eucharistic action at the altar of God.

Study outline

What role does baptism play in the life of faith?

Baptism introduces us into the family of God, the Christian community

The rite of early times signifies this fully
    New Christians were received by the community at the Easter Vigil
    Parents were the sponsors of the candidate
The community is the church, the body of Christ
    The risen Lord is still in our midst
    Baptism initiates each member into the mystery of Christ

Christ joins us to himself in carrying on his mission in the world

Christ was sent by the Father
    To acknowledge the heavenly Father
    To bring men to fuller life through himself

We share the missionary aim of the church
  We are to worship
  We are commissioned to the apostolate
Christ touches us, marks us
  We are ordained to share in Christ's priesthood
  We are sent from the altar to transform the lives of men through the
    vision and charity of Christ

Through baptism we are introduced into a new way of life

The Father truly becomes our father
A personal transformation occurs in baptism
  The new birth is not an elevation but a "divinization"
  We are opened to a new way of life with the Trinity

Baptism is an orientation of the Eucharistic action.

The Eucharist, the new covenant, is the fulfillment of baptism
Each participation is a deeper entry into the mystery of the death,
  burial, and resurrection of Christ
  In baptism we enter into this mystery for the first time
  The "rites of initiation" culminate in the Eucharist

Study questions

1 If, as the Constitution on the Sacred Liturgy indicates, the revised
  sacramental sign of baptism is to make the sign more readily understood, what elements need to be emphasized in the proposed rite?
2 Why is the fitting celebration of the Easter Vigil of prime importance
  in renewing a genuine Christian life?
3 Contrast the development of the life of faith of an adult convert with
  that of a person baptized in infancy
4 At one time baptism was a self-contained subject in a religious program. How should the reality of baptism permeate the program?

Further study

Sacred Scripture: John 3:5-7, 4:5-42; Acts 1:4-5; Romans 6:3-5.
Charles Davis. *Sacraments of Initiation: Baptism and Confirmation.*
  New York: Sheed and Ward, 1964.
Lucien De Bontridder. "The Bible and the Sacraments of Christian
  Initiation," in *Teaching the Sacraments and Morality,* edited by Mark
  J. Link, S.J. Chicago: Loyola University Press, 1965. Pp. 29-44.
Augustine Grail, O.P., and others. *Baptism in the New Testament.*
  Baltimore: Helicon Press, 1964.
Ignatius Hunt, O.S.B. *Baptism.* (Doctrinal Pamphlet Series) Glen Rock:
  Paulist Press, 1962.
Aimé Georges Martimort. *The Signs of the New Covenant.* Collegeville:
  Liturgical Press, 1963.

Faith
and penance

The commitment made at baptism is meant to last throughout our lives and to manifest itself in gradually developing faith. Adult faith finds expression in all the attitudes, behavior, and situations of our Christian lives.

The problem here is that though we know what we are supposed to be, we are not always that way. We are human, and for all of us that means experiencing weakness and sin. Though we try to live as Christians ought, we fail in many ways. In the course of our daily lives we allow ourselves to be separated from the mystery of Christ, to become involved in many situations which are not compatible with devout Christian faith. A measure of infidelity enters our lives. At baptism we swore to be faithful to Christ, to God the Father, to our fellow Christians, and to the task that we share. But in many situations we are not faithful and must constantly accuse ourselves of failing to fulfill the commitment of our baptism.

Christ foresaw this when he was in our midst in visible form. He saw his own apostles yield to temptation, and he knew that Christianity must provide for the forgiveness of men. That is why he left with us the sacrament of penance as a means of reconciling us to himself, to the Father, and to one another. This, with the Eucharist, is the sacrament which probably functions most frequently in the life of the ordinary Christian. Week after week and month after month we need to come to Christ to ask his forgiveness.

Penance, however, is not just a seeking of forgiveness from Christ and God the Father. It involves reconciliation with the Christian community of which we have been unfaithful members. When we were baptized as Christians, we promised something to the other members of the Christian community. We said that we wanted to accept this group's objectives and its mission. Then we were unfaithful in fulfilling our mission. We need constant reconciliation with the Christian community through the sacrament of penance. The priest delegated by the community to hear confessions accepts us back into full, authentic membership; he reconciles us, as individuals and in community, to one another, to Christ, and to the heavenly Father. The sacrament of penance was given by Christ, because being man himself he recognized our weakness, sinfulness, constant infidelity, and need for forgiveness and reconciliation.

The night the sacrament of penance was instituted, the night of the Resurrection itself, the apostles were gathered together in the upper room. They were frightened and disturbed, and they were worried, not just because of the Jews who might come, but because they did not know how they stood with Christ. They had abandoned him when he most needed them. When he was seized in the garden they fled. Peter, who followed for a while, finally denied him. How did Christ regard these friends who had failed him?

As the disciples sat talking about these things, suddenly Christ was there in their midst in all his risen glory. There were no words of blame or accusation. Christ said simply, "Peace be to you!" (John 20:19). This was what he wanted for his followers. "Peace be to you!" he said and he gave them the Spirit forever in the sacrament of penance. Again he said: "Peace be to you! . . . Receive the Holy Spirit; whose sins you shall forgive, they are forgiven them; and whose sins you shall retain, they are retained" (John 20:21-23). The power to forgive sin was given to the apostles so that they and their successors might pass down even to our own day the calm, peace, and joy of Christ in his resurrection. Christ wanted to share these with us, and so the atmosphere of the sacrament of penance is that of the Resurrection.

We often forget, however, the connection between penance and the action of the Eucharist. The night of the Last Supper, before Christ's gift of his body and blood, John's Gospel tells us that Christ washed the feet of his disciples. This showed them that he was in their midst serving them; it also showed the purification that was needed before one could really partake fully of the Eucharistic Banquet. This is where the sacrament of penance fits into our lives. The Eucharist is an action of self-giving. When we bring our gifts, we and Christ give ourselves to one another. The problem is that this action of self-giving, on our part, is not always genuine. We are fulfilling our baptismal promise, dedicating ourselves to Christ, to worship, to work in the church. Yet, as individuals and as a community, do we really deserve to stand around the altar and say this? Can we really say to God the Father in all honesty: "I am giving you myself entirely. I really am dedicating myself to the service of the church, to the service of mankind, so that I can leave the Eucharistic table and take part in changing the world"? We have to admit that alone we cannot say this. We hedge on our commitment time and time again. We deny our dedication. We do not give ourselves totally. What we need before we come to the Eucharist is some sort of purification, something that will enable us to say these things with full honesty.

That "something" is the sacrament of penance. We cannot by ourselves ever honestly say that we are giving ourselves completely. But we can say it in terms of the fact that Christ works in our lives in the sacrament of penance, carrying on a constant purification which makes us less unworthy to make this statement. In this way we can live out the reality of our self-giving.

This is how the sacraments of penance and the Eucharist are interrelated. The Eucharist speaks of a going out into the apostolate, fulfilling our baptismal promises to worship and participate in the mission of Christ. Christ says to us as he said to his disciples, "As the Father has sent me, I also send you" (John 20:21). Though we are sent to transform the lives of men by the love of Christ—which works, lives, and finds expression in our own Christian love—the vision that we give men often is not of Christ but of a distorted Christian view. Our love is denied to the people who need it. We need not consider only those in foreign lands who need Christ; the people in the "inner core" of our cities and those who live around us also need our love. Their salvation is dependent, to some extent, upon whether we love generously. Yet we have to say in all honesty, humility, and repentance that we do not always love this way. As a result apostolic work does not always have the effectiveness it should have. But if Christ himself comes into our lives, straightens us out, strengthens us, repairs the inadequacy of our love by his own power, we can participate effectively in the action of redemption. The sacrament of penance helps us to become redeemed "redeemers." It gives us the power of Christ, working to purify and to integrate our lives and our love. Only thus purified can we effectively join him in the work of the transformation of human life.

The sacrament of penance is really a profound profession of our faith. Its important function in the formation of faith is that through it our faith matures. As we recognize our need for the salvation that comes from Christ in this sacrament, we realize that we must trust and depend on him. This is a profession of our faith. This is really acknowledging our weakness and need. This is accepting Christ's gift of redemption which empowers us to fulfill our baptismal commitment. This is living with integrity.

Sadly, Christians do not completely appreciate the sacrament in these terms. They do not realize that there must be something to lead up to the sacrament of penance, something we call conscience. Its formation is an important element in the larger reality of the formation of faith. Parents and teachers should for that reason be vitally concerned with it. In order to utilize the benefits of the sacrament, penance must be preceded by penitence. Christians ought not to live their lives as perpetual children, always needing explicit directions and having constantly to be reproved and corrected. They should develop a personal awareness of what it means to live as Christians.

An adult conscience is not formed by reading a list of sins. Too often instruction in this matter consists in having people memorize the commandments of God and the church. But people can know all the categories of sins and not understand what it means to be truly Christian. We must live out our baptism by accepting responsibility for being Christian. An adult Christian is one who really believes that his faith is to be lived with integrity; that accepting baptism means living with responsibility to others, to oneself, and to the kingdom of God.

The acceptance of such responsibility stems from genuine love: love of God, love of one's fellowmen, love of oneself. We must ask ourselves Have I denied love? Have I denied love to myself? Have I forgotten that I am loved by God, that I am someone with identity and dignity? I should live as though I am loved and accept the fact that I am. Have I denied love to my fellow Christians? Have I been so self-centered that I have not gone out to them, nor seen their needs, nor responded to them, nor given of myself so that their lives may be fuller and more Christian? Perhaps I have even denied love to Christ and to God the Father. I may have become so engrossed in the "practical" pursuits of life that I have forgotten the friendship that exists between God the Father and me, between Christ and me. I may have taken neither the time nor the effort to pray. The formation of an adult conscience, then, is more than being concerned with a list of precepts; it is accepting full responsibility for life.

How is one really to practice this sacrament? First, we should not approach the sacrament of penance with fear. It ought to be a thing of calm. Tension and fear lest we forget to confess every sin have no place here. Penance is meant to be the honest adult statement of each individual's own particular need for redemption. Perhaps I am too impatient with people, or perhaps I do not trust God enough. Instead of having the confidence and the freedom that should characterize a Christian, I am fearful, hesitant, and impatient. In the sacrament of penance I state this, and through the absolution redemption comes to me for my specific faith need. My confessing forms part of the sacrament itself.

Another aspect of the practice of penance is frequently misunderstood: the matter of feeling. Many Christians believe that when they approach this sacrament they must have experienced deep within themselves an emotion of sorrow.

Sometimes this is just not possible. It may be that what I have done since the last confession has not been earthshakingly wrong, and I cannot feel terribly shattered about it. The fact that I do not feel sorrow-stricken does not indicate that my confession of sins has not been genuine; nor is it worth any less. The important thing is not the feeling but the decision. As a Christian, as an adult, I must look at my life and admit the deficiencies in it. I must decide with God's help to do everything possible to remove these deficiencies from my life. Without becoming unduly guilt-ridden I must be sorry that I have been weak and tell Christ so. I must ask for forgiveness, know it is given, and realize that as I am meant to live in an atmosphere of serenity, I must keep my soul in peace. When the priest says to me as I leave the confessional, "Go in peace," I must take his blessing as a literal admonition. I must learn to live out the decision of my baptism.

Though we often fail to live up to our baptismal commitment to genuine worship and authentic apostolate, we should always recall that Christ has given us the gift of forgiveness and reconciliation. Only through it can we share in the Eucharistic celebration with integrity. Only then can we as adults with fully formed consciences share in the Christian apostolate.

Study outline

The sacrament of penance is a profound profession of faith

The sacrament of penance continues the redemptive work begun in baptism

The commitment of baptism is meant to express itself in an ever-developing adult faith
We all experience weakness and sin, failures in fidelity to Christ and the Father
Christ provided for the forgiveness of man in the sacrament of penance, an instrument of forgiveness
    We constantly need to ask forgiveness of Christ
    We need reconciliation with the Christian community
The Resurrection is the atmosphere of the sacrament of penance
    The sacrament was instituted on the night of the Resurrection in a context of peace and joy
    Christ gives the spirit of peace to those seeking acceptance

The sacrament of penance is related to the Eucharistic Banquet

Purification before the Eucharist was signified in the washing of the feet

The Eucharist is a sacrament of self-giving, dedication to worship and the work of the church
Before the Eucharist we need purification to render worthy the gift of ourselves
The Eucharist involves a commitment to transform the lives of men
Often we give a distorted Christian vision and refuse to love
Our apostolic work is ineffective unless Christ strengthens and redeems us, redeemed "redeemers"

The formation of an adult conscience is an important element in the life of faith

The formation is not a learning of a list of sins
The real formation is an awareness, a living out of baptism by accepting responsibility for self, others, the kingdom of God
The key question in preparation for the sacrament is "Have I denied love?"

The sacrament is to be used in a mature way

It is to be approached with calm, not fear
Here is an honest, adult statement of a need for redemption, trust, freedom
Redemption is given each for his specific needs
The sacrament of penance is not a matter of feeling
The *emotion* of sorrow is not essential
It is rather a *decision* to live out baptism
"Go in peace" is to be taken seriously

Study questions

1 What is the role of the sacrament of penance in the lives of young Catholics today?
2 What elements of this sacrament need greater understanding and emphasis?
3 Do we have a living awareness of a) the natural place of this sacrament in a life of friendship with Christ, b) its resurrection context, c) its power to heal our break with the community, d) its power to make us effective "redeemers," e) its true relationship to the Eucharist, f) the real meaning of an adult conscience?
4 What can we and our students do in the parish, school, and religion class to deepen our understanding and improve our participation in this sacrament?

Further study

Sacred Scripture: Mark 2:10-12; John 20:21-23.
Paul Anciaux. *The Sacrament of Penance.* New York: Sheed and Ward, 1962.

Thomas M. Finn, C.S.P. *Penance.* (Doctrinal Pamphlet Series) Glen Rock: Paulist Press, 1962.

Xavier Lefebvre, S.J., and Louis Perin, S.J. *Going to God.* New York: P. J. Kenedy and Sons, 1964.

Aimé Georges Martimort. *The Signs of the New Covenant.* Collegeville: Liturgical Press, 1963.

Madeleine Mélot. "Preparing the Child for the Sacrament of Penance," in *Teaching the Sacraments and Morality,* edited by Mark J. Link, S.J. Chicago: Loyola University Press, 1964. Pp. 89-95.

Bernhard Poschmann. *Penance and the Anointing of the Sick.* New York: Herder and Herder, 1964.

A. M. Roguet, O.P. *Christ Acts through the Sacraments.* Collegeville: Liturgical Press, 1954.

The Community of Saint-Séverin. *Confession.* Notre Dame: Fides Publishers, 1959.

John Sheerin, C.S.P. *The Sacrament of Freedom.* Milwaukee: Bruce Publishing Company, 1961.

Adrienne von Speyr. *Confession.* New York: Herder and Herder, 1964.

Faith
and the
Eucharist

In discussing faith, its nature, and above all its formation, one point has been central: "Faith then depends on hearing" (Romans 10:17). In other words, if we never hear about God the Father, Christ, the Holy Spirit, and the mystery of our transformation in grace, our sonship, then it is impossible for us to have faith. We may be people of good will; we may without knowing it possess grace which draws us to God. Yet we cannot really have a clear, living faith because no one has told us what that is. One of the important prerequisites for faith is coming into contact with the word of God. We must listen to the word of God in Holy Scripture. We must listen to the word of God in the context of sacrament.

Of all the sacraments, the most important by far is the Eucharistic action of the Mass. It is in the Eucharist that we speak our faith most fully and where Christ himself speaks to us most graphically. It is the supreme context for the formation of our faith.

At the present time the church is in a period of liturgical renewal, evidenced by the Constitution on the Sacred Liturgy.

In this document the Second Vatican Council seeks to clarify for us the meaning of the Eucharistic action. At the risk of oversimplification and undue repetition, let us review how the Mass feeds our faith.

The first portion of the Mass is what we call the Liturgy of the Word of God—restrictively, of course, for the whole of it is really his word, since all of it speaks to us. This scriptural word, however, has special prominence in the early portion. The actual reading of the word of God in Scripture and its explanation follows the entrance rite and precedes the Liturgy of the Eucharist in its full context: the bringing of the gifts, the Offertory; the Eucharistic Prayer, which we sometimes call the Canon; and finally, the Eucharistic Banquet, sometimes referred to as Holy Communion.

In considering each part of the Eucharistic action separately, we start with the entrance rite. Usually the people have already assembled. On certain solemn occasions some of them can also be in the procession, although nowadays this is not very practicable. The priest comes from the sacristy (sometimes from the back of the church) and proceeds toward the altar. When he reaches it he bows to recite the prayer known as the Confiteor, acknowledging the fact that he and all the congregation are unworthy to approach the altar. This part of the sacrament speaks of the faith of the participants and expresses their desire and intention to worship God the Father in union with Christ.

Not so obvious is the truth that Christ is already in their midst. Otherwise, those present would not be a Christian community. The members accept Christ's presence as fact and acknowledge their unworthiness. On behalf of the community, then, the priest approaches the altar and bows in the action of the Confiteor. This is followed by the "Lord, have mercy" and the Prayer, sometimes called the Collect. Then follows the liturgy of the spoken word of Scripture. This opens as the lector from the congregation reads the Epistle and the Gradual. Then a second priest or the celebrant reads the Gospel. As we listen to the reading of the Scripture we have to remember that this is a faith context. These are not simply human words; the one reading is proclaiming the word of Christ himself. It is he who speaks through the reader, and as we listen we are really in contact with Christ. The word of Christ is directed toward us for the formation of our faith. There are many things in Scripture, in the Epistle and the Gospel at Mass, that we do not understand perfectly. Some of these perhaps were clearer to the people who lived when the Gospels and Epistles were originally written. We need the explanation which is provided in what we call the Homily or the Sermon. In it the Scripture is explained and applied to our present situation.

This gives us a context for professing our belief, our acceptance. We do this in the Creed which we recite together, particularly on Sundays, and in the recently reintroduced Prayer of the Faithful. These prayers are a response in faith, because the word of Scripture tells us that the God is a father and that Christ is here. Trusting in the fatherhood of God and Christ's love for us, in the Prayer of the Faithful we speak our needs. We pray in our own behalf; we pray for those in authority in the church and civil government; we pray for the poor and the afflicted; we pray for all the needs of mankind. Prayer is a statement of our faith, of our trust in the fact that God the Father will hear these prayers and that Christ, who has told us that whatever we ask in his name will be granted, is really faithful to this promise.

We move on toward the Liturgy of the Eucharist. The preparatory stage concerns our gifts. (Here it would be good to recall that as we come into the church, if we intend to receive Communion, we place our host in the basket.) At this point in the Mass two members of the community, or more if they are needed, carry the bread and wine to the altar. This says that these are our gifts. We brought them. And the bringing of gifts is a way of showing that we want to give ourselves to God; it is an enacted word; it is a dramatization of our intent, our faith, our acceptance of Christ, and our willingness to commit ourselves to him. These gifts are placed on the altar, as a sign that they are now handed over to God. They belong to him. In a sense by being put in this place they are rendered sacred. Since we are represented by this bread and wine, *we* are set aside, dedicated to God. We do not simply belong to ourselves in complete independence anymore. We have given ourselves to God and to his service.

Another thing which the bringing of food and drink says is that we are going to have a meal. We are prepared now to partake of the sacred covenant meal in union with Christ and the Father. The sharing of sustenance binds us to God, links us to him in a family situation, dedicates us to him. He is accepting us and binding himself to us also. This meal reminds us of the one shared by Christ and his disciples two thousand years ago, the night before he died. There is a real, historical connection between that dinner and the one which we now take together in the Eucharist.

When the gifts have been laid on the altar, we proceed to the focal portion, in a sense, of the Mass: the Eucharistic Prayer, the Canon. It extends from the Preface—when the priest says, "Lift up your hearts. Let us give thanks to God,"—to the Little Elevation. This giving of thanks is extremely important. Thankfulness is the most basic attitude that we Christians are meant to have. The bringing of bread and wine expresses our thanksgiving to God the Father for sending his Son to redeem us. How naturally, then, the thanksgiving leads to the Consecration of the Mass, where God through the words of institution ("This is my body . . . this is my blood") actually changes our gifts of bread and wine into Christ himself. The gift which we have brought is now transformed so that it can be a gift to us. This action speaks of God's sending his Son here for our sake. Just as the bread and wine are transformed, "christianized" if you will, so also are we who are signified by that bread and wine changed. And with continued participation in this action we are increasingly conformed to the image and likeness of Christ himself.

The Canon ends with the close of the Eucharistic Prayer, when the priest raises the chalice and the host and says, "Through him and with him and in him are given to you, God the almighty Father, in the unity of the Holy Spirit, all honor and all glory for ever and ever"; and the people say, "Amen." This is their action; they have their part in it. Through their assent to it the priest's prayer becomes that of the entire Christian community.

The final portion of the action of the Mass, the Eucharistic Banquet or Communion, follows. It is linked with the Eucharistic Prayer by the Our Father. And this is an extremely appropriate link, for in the Eucharistic Banquet God the Father gives us his Son as our brother, as a source of life. By means of the

Eucharist we identify ourselves with Christ and, therefore, accept God the Father as our father. To make this clear, as we approach this portion of the liturgy and before receiving the Body of Christ, we recite together the Our Father.

When the priest gives us the Body of Christ the action speaks of Christ's gift of himself to us. In our ordinary human friendships this is the most profound thing that we can give another person. Much more valuable than money or anything else is the gift of oneself, and this Christ gives in the form of food.

The Eucharistic action also says, however, that Christ comes to us in order that we may live, that we may have the very life which he possesses now as the risen Lord. This is why he takes the form of food, to manifest externally his coming to us. He purposely comes under the sign of food so that it can speak to us of his intent to make us live, and to live as fully as he himself lives. On Christ's side, then, it is a giving of himself as a source of life. Sent from his father, he speaks of the Father's love for us.

From our point of view, the receiving of Christ as food is a very important profession of our faith. We stand up of our own free choice and walk forward to Communion, where we encounter Christ and receive him. We take him into our own lives, into our very selves as a sign of the fact that we want to be united with him. In doing this we have deeply committed ourselves to Christ and to all he stands for. We can only receive the friendship of another by giving our own. So it is when we receive Christ and his love for us; we are committing ourselves to love him.

Faith in the New Testament is essentially the acceptance of Christ, which has its full context only in the Eucharistic action. When Christ comes to me I not only accept what I have heard about him, but I accept him in the fullness of his being. This is the high point of all faith. Faith is a deeply personal experience. It is not merely saying Yes to words, the catechism, explanations; faith is the experience of being a Christian. United with my fellow Christians around the altar, praising God the Father, with Christ in our midst—this is what it means to be a Christian.

It is clear, then, that we ought to participate in the Eucharist. It is not enough just to be there. Nor can we even be "following at a distance." If it is our intention really to experience Christianity, we must understand the structure of the Mass and what takes place in it. This is a meal, the proclamation of God's Word, and our response. It unites us, because we are acknowledging our one Father in heaven, receiving together the one body of Christ, and committing ourselves individually and in community to Christ. All these truths we have to understand with increasing depth and accuracy if our faith is mature.

To put it another way, just taking part in the Mass is not enough; our participation must be intelligent, generous, and therefore informed. Today when we have the opportunity of participating in this way because of the clarification of the liturgy, we must make every effort to see that we and others are prepared to understand the action of the Eucharist. The action itself helps. The Homily during the Mass should further our understanding.

But we also have to read and discuss and perhaps have someone explain the significance of our actions. Fortunately, in most places this is being done in conjunction with the changes in the liturgy. There has been a great deal of explanation given the people so that we understand what is taking place. This is what the church desires, as is clear in the Constitution on the Sacred Liturgy. The church does not want us to attend the celebration of the Eucharist as silent spectators. It wants us to hear the Word of God and to respond to it. It wants us to receive in gratitude and thanksgiving the body of Christ in Holy Communion. It wants us to offer ourselves so that in the experience we will learn what it means to live as a sacred, priestly people, who in faith give our entire lives to God the Father.

Study outline

The Eucharistic action is the supreme context for the formation of faith. Each part of the structure is a "word directed to the people of God." Through the changes in the liturgy the church is trying to clarify the meaning of each.

Structure	Meaning
Liturgy of the Word	
Entrance Rite Procession	We gather as believers and speak our intention to worship the Father with Christ.
Confiteor	Christ is in our midst, present where we are.
"Lord, have mercy" Prayer	We accept his presence and acknowledge our unworthiness.

The Word of God
  Epistle
  Gradual
  Gospel
	The reader proclaims the word of Christ who speaks to us. The word is directed to us for our faith.
	The word is applied to our present situation.

Creed	We profess our acceptance of and assent to the word.
Prayer of the Faithful	We respond in faith: the Father is our father, Christ our loving redeemer; we pray in trust for our needs.
Liturgy of the Eucharist	
Bringing of Gifts to the Altar	We signify our willingness to commit ourselves to Christ. The enacted word indicates that we, with them, are set aside; we belong to God. In the covenant meal we dedicate ourselves to God and are accepted by him.
Eucharistic Prayer (extends from Preface to the closing Amen)	Thanksgiving is the basic attitude of one who believes—thanksgiving for Christ our redeemer and for this Eucharistic action.
Consecration	The bread and wine are changed into Christ, our gift into his; we are transformed.
Amen	The people's action makes the prayer that of the entire community.
Eucharistic Banquet Our Father	We profess our acceptance of Christ from the Father as our source of life.
Reception of the Body of Christ	His coming as food tells us that Christ will give us his life. (The most valuable gift in friendship is oneself.) In this profession of faith we show our desire for identification with Christ and accept *him,* not only what we know *about* him.

Faith is a deep personal experience which show us what it is to be a Christian, united with others and Christ, praising the Father. It is important that we participate actively, intelligently, and generously in the Eucharistic action. In this experience of offering ourselves we learn how to live as a priestly people.

Study questions

1 Have the changes in the liturgy thus far really helped clarify the meaning of the Mass?
2 What effort must be undertaken if the real change, that of our hearts, is to occur?

Further study

The Constitution on the Sacred Liturgy of the Second Vatican Council. Glen Rock: Paulist Press, 1964.

Charles Davis. *Liturgy and Doctrine.* New York: Sheed and Ward, 1960.

William J. Leonard, S.J. *New Horizons in Catholic Worship.* Wichita: Liturgical Commission, 1964.

Pastoral Directory on the Mass. Chicago: Liturgical Commission, 1965.

Frederick R. McManus, editor. *The Revival of the Liturgy.* New York: Herder and Herder, 1963.

J. Richard Quinn. *God's People at Mass.* New York: Benziger Brothers, 1964.

Faith and the catechist: Introducing the risen Christ

What must the catechist—that is to say, the one who is educating toward faith—do in order that faith come to fullness, clarity, and maturity? The "catechist" generally is not simply the individual who instructs children formally in their faith in a classroom. In a larger context, parents forming the faith of their children, older brothers and sisters working with the younger ones in the family, young people in discussion are catechists, as much as the teacher of a formal class. How should one be a catechist? How does one go about educating and instructing in faith? This is a unique educational experience.

Education is always a difficult task. It involves forming people's thoughts and values, leading them to freedom, decision, and mature personal judgment. But if this is difficult in ordinary circumstances, it is uniquely so in religious education. There we deal with a context and a content beyond any other kind of education in the home or in the school.

Faith concerns an encounter with a person. It is not accepting formulae or words or propositions; it is not repeating truths that have been given in the catechism. Faith is the acceptance of a person, and the person is Christ. It is precisely this that makes catechesis, religious instruction, such a unique thing. In other teaching we can explain the contents of textbook to a child and feel that we have succeeded if he can give us back that understanding.

But if we teach catechism this way, we have not succeeded, because the essential process of religious instruction is that of introducing the child to the person of Christ. In a sense what we have to do is tell the child about Christ and all that Christ means, and thus "lead" him step by step to an "introduction" to Christ. We must say, "This is Christ." Once we have done that, our function as religious teachers is, as it were, to retreat, to allow the child to become acquainted with Christ by himself, and in that situation to have his faith formed. What is true of Christ is true of God the Father. We must introduce the child to this person who is the father of Christ, and here too it is not sufficient simply to talk *about* God the Father. We must personally introduce the child to him. Obviously, I have to describe the Father. I have to tell the child about him and who he is. But always I must lead him to the personal acceptance of the father of our Lord Jesus Christ.

Christ, however, must be the center and foundation of all our religious teaching. Everything we talk about must bear a relationship to Christ. Moreover, it is extremely important that we talk about Christ as he is—that is to say, as the present Christ, the risen Christ, not as if he were only a historical figure. We must be very clear in talking to a child or an adult that the Christ about whom we are speaking lives now and not in some previous age. He is present in our world, the situation in which we find ourselves. Christ is now in his risen state. He is glorified, has conquered death, and is triumphant.

This does not mean that every class that we teach must always speak specifically of Christ. A class about one of the command-ments or about the sacrament of anointing, for example, need not start with a discussion about Christ. Rather, I as a teacher must be so thoroughly convinced of the reality of Christ risen and present that, without adverting to it consciously, I am constantly assuming that he is present and risen. As the child listens to me he gains the impression, without my having to argue the point, that this is so, because that is always the way I talk about Christ. Christ must be the background, the context— you might almost say the "atmosphere"—in which everything else that I deal with and explain is treated. This is essential to any genuine Christian catechesis. It must be profoundly Christ-centered, Christ-dominated. Everything I talk about concerns the one to whom I am gradually leading the child, so that the time comes when his own consciousness begins to appreciate Christ's presence and the fact that he is risen. When I have taught this way, my catechesis and religious teaching is really valid. This is more important than discussing this technique or that, whether to use visual aids or a tape. The important thing is that Christ be central in the message.

The reason this is absolutely essential is that religious instruction is not meant to terminate simply with information. Something much deeper is intended in valid Christian catechesis. The teacher must lead even a young person to conversion. You may ask what conversion can mean to a little child. Fundamentally it means that wherever we are in our understanding of Christ, and in our appreciation of him, we always have to move forward to a deeper understanding and acceptance of Christ. To that extent there is always a need for conversion. This is what we are trying to achieve in our religious instruction. The child or the young person should turn ever more fully toward Christ. If he does convert this way and continues to move closer to Christ, he is being taught the right way; but if conversion does not come, his religious instruction is very inadequate.

What is involved is not a conversion to acting a certain way or resolving to do certain things. It is a conversion to a personal relationship with Christ. It can never be stressed too strongly that this is the essence, the very heart of faith. Unless a personal relationship between the child and Christ is established, there can be no genuine faith. The conversion involved is meant to lead to a deep personal relatedness. We are seeking a conversion profoundly personal, so that the consciousness, the love, and even the emotional life and the imagination of the convert turn ever more completely to Christ. When that happens the one being educated has become a thoroughly convinced and living Christian. This is what we want, that Christianity be deep in those with whom we deal so that the mystery and the reality of Christ is uppermost in their whole life experience.

This leads to something else important in our role as catechists. If we are going to lead those whom we teach to a genuine religious turning toward Christ, we must be sure that it is toward him that we are pointing. To lead them to Christ, then, we must lead them to Christ as he really is. Our constant task in religious education is one of helping others toward a more accurate understanding of who and what Christ is. This raises a problem for catechists. We must be very sure that our own understanding of Christ is accurate. If I am to take a child by the hand and lead him, saying, "This is Christ," I have to know the true Christ. I cannot lead him to an image which I myself have created. That is why the catechist must study and pray: to be sure that the Christ about whom he speaks to the child is the real one.

Children need at times to have corrected certain pictures they have of Christ. Someone may have told them that Christ is always watching them, causing them to fear Christ (tragic for a little child). Christ may have been highly sentimentalized instead of having been depicted in all his mature dignity and simple human greatness. Do not underestimate children. They have a capacity to appraise individuals. If we are going to have them form a judgment of Christ as someone appealing, we must be sure to describe Christ accurately, so that the image they have of him corresponds to the reality of the Man who is also God. All our teaching should clarify, correct, delineate, describe, and present as living and vital the reality of the risen Christ. We want to introduce these children to Christ, so that he will be the object of their faith and love, so that they will turn increasingly toward him; that is to say, be converted.

This sounds like a rather frightening task, and in many respects it is. It is a great responsibility. Fortunately an invaluable aid has been given us, without which we could not hope to accomplish what we have just described. It is Christ's own description of himself in the pages of the New Testament Scriptures, far more reliable than our own interpretation. One of the primary objectives of all our religious education must be to lead the child to the Scriptures. It is true that a little child cannot understand much about Scripture yet, but we can begin to instill in him an all-important attitude toward it. It is the Word of God, and not in a watered-down, inadequate sense.

It is true that hundreds of years ago God spoke to men who wrote down what he said. But the full truth is that even now Christ speaks to us in the Bible. Scripture still is his word. It takes a long time for people to appreciate this. Unless children are convinced that this is so as they go into young adulthood and then into full maturity, unless they form that attitude, Scripture will always remain for them just another book about Christ.

The second step in leading them to Scripture is to direct them to the message. Today there is a great deal of interest in Scripture, and often talks given on the subject, even classes, can tend to become lost in the details of historical dates, geographical locations, and many names. A certain amount of background is needed, but what is important is the religious message contained in Scripture. We must tell children and young people what the message is. For hundreds of years God has been trying to tell us who he is, how he wants to bring us to himself, what we must do in order to achieve union with him. This is the marvelous mystery of the message of God's Word: his love for us. God reveals himself to us as he speaks in Sacred Scripture, and as the child hears it God the Father, the risen Christ, and the Holy Spirit become living realities for him. If we have led him in our religious instruction to the point of reading and understanding Scripture this way, we have given him a priceless heritage for the rest of his life. We have made it possible for him to become truly and fully a Christian.

Yet, there is an even fuller action to which we must lead the child: the action of the Eucharist. This is where all our religious instruction must end. As teachers of the Word of God we must lead the young believer toward an intelligent activity in the Eucharistic action of the Mass. This is why he was baptized: to participate in this action; and it is only here that he encounters the adequate object of his faith. We must take the child by the hand in religious instruction and lead him to Christ in the Eucharist. Having brought him to this place, we can leave him with the reality of Christ, his Lord and Master.

The action of the Mass is central in all our catechetical work. Everything about which Scripture speaks and all our explanations about Scripture point toward it. Scripture is the word of God describing the mystery of God's working in New and Old

Testament times. That mystery finds its actuality in its continuation, in the Eucharist. All our teaching about Scripture should point to and find its fulfillment in the Eucharist because our catechesis is meant to lead our students to Christ. It is the Eucharistic action which makes Christ present in the clearest, most effective form. There the Christian community can really come into contact with the present, living, risen Christ. If we do not lead students toward the Eucharistic action, we are merely telling them about swimming on dry land. We do not give them an opportunity to encounter the experience. Christian faith grows in Christian experience, and the place where the Christian is meant to experience Christ is the Eucharist. There we must lead students if they are to have a personal encounter with Christ.

How do we prepare the child or the young adult for a personal encounter with Christ? We do it by explaining the Eucharist to him in terms of his own life experiences. What has a child experienced? In the family, the home, he has learned what it means to give and to receive. He knows what it means to eat with the family and to be kind toward others and to be loved. These are precisely the experiences that the teacher draws on to teach the child how to come to the Eucharist and to bring himself as a gift. Here the child can show his love for Christ by participating in the Eucharistic Banquet. For him this situation really means meeting Christ, encountering and coming to know him, so it is here our teaching finds its fulfillment.

We must talk to our students about Christ as present and living. We must describe him as he is. Then we must lead them to the Eucharist to meet Christ. Only if we do this will our catechesis be a success.

Study outline

What must the catechist do to help bring faith to maturity?

Religious education is a unique education situation

Content and context extend beyond the usual educational process
  A mere understanding is insufficient
  Faith is an encounter, an acceptance of a person
The catechist must introduce the child to Christ and to the father of Christ

Christ must be the center and foundation of religious instruction

Christ must be presented as he is, glorified, risen, present

The child gains an impression from the teacher's conviction: the sense of Christ risen and present is the atmosphere surrounding all explanations

The instruction is not meant to terminate in information, but to lead the person to conversion

We are always in need of a deeper understanding and acceptance of Christ

We are concerned with conversion, not as a way of acting, but as a turning of one's life toward Christ

We need to help young people to a more accurate understanding of the true Christ

The primary, invaluable aid to an accurate description of Christ is his own word about himself

We must lead the child to Scripture

We must lead the child to the message of Scripture

We tend to get lost in details

What is important is what God is saying to us, the message of his love for us

Religious instructions must end in the action of the Eucharist

The action of the Mass is central

Scripture is the word of God, describing the mystery which is continued in the Eucharist

The sacrament makes Christ present in clearest form

In it the Christian community comes into contact with the present, risen Lord

The Eucharist should be explained in terms of the child's experience

The experience of family life—giving and receiving of gifts, eating, and loving—should be used

The child learns to participate in the Eucharistic Banquet with the present, living Christ

Study questions

1 In what way does a personal relationship with Christ depend upon sound knowledge? How does depth of understanding follow from a personal relationship with Christ?

2 How can the study of the Old Testament be soundly Christ-centered?

3 What is the full dimension of a catechist's work in leading the student to Christ? What is the many-sided preparation necessary for a catechist?

4 How can we make participation in the paschal mystery the crown of religious education?

Further study

Pierre Babin. "Main Lines of Catechesis," *Crisis of Faith*. New York: Herder and Herder, 1963. Pp. 195-221.

Sofia Cavalletti and Gianna Gobbi. *Teaching Doctrine and Liturgy: the Montessori Approach.* New York: Alba House, 1964.

Sister Michael, O.L.V.M. *Communicating the Mystery.* Huntington: Our Sunday Visitor, 1963.

Roger Poelman. "The Paschal Plan of God," in *Teaching the Sacraments and Morality,* edited by Mark J. Link, S.J. Chicago: Loyola University Press, 1965. Pp. 9-19.

Gerard S. Sloyan, editor. *Modern Catechetics.* New York: The Macmillan Company, 1963.

Marcel Van Caster, S.J. *The Structure of Catechetics.* New York: Herder and Herder, 1965.

Faith and
the catechist:
Sense of community

Faith is an acceptance of Christ in the context of Scripture, sacrament, and the life of the church. As it is vital and personal, it is meant to transform the lives of young people and adults. This lays a difficult task upon those parents or teachers who are entrusted with the religious formation of the young. The center of all our attention, the whole atmosphere of our teaching, must be the reality of Christ. This Divine Person became man like one of us, lived a human experience like our own about two thousand years ago, died, and is now with us, risen. This Christ is the one to whom we must lead young and old if their faith is to be a genuinely vital human experience.

Two things, especially, have to be kept in mind in teaching: Christ and the Christian community. Having considered the first, let us turn to the second. The effective teacher of faith must place his teaching within the context of the community called the church.

First of all, this community of faith is truly a family situation. It is not primarily an organization, nor is it a series of *dos* and *don'ts* in structures and activities. Basically the church is a people, the people of God. This is what we must convey to those who form the community of faith. We must introduce young people to faith within the context of the church. We must bring these young people into the atmosphere of their own identification with the Christian community. What must characterize their realization of all the religious instruction is the fact that they are members of this community. The effective catechist creates in young people a sense of belonging to a family.

This requires more than merely telling them that the church is a family. Something more subtle, more profound, is involved: real awareness, a sense, a conviction of belonging to this group which is the community of faith. Admittedly this goal is not easy to attain. Anyone who has worked in the area of religious formation and religious education knows how difficult it is to have students pass beyond the stage of a mere verbal understanding of this concept. Students use the word "church," but to them too often it simply means the building or that vague structure which includes the bishops, priests, and religious. That is the church. But they do not identify themselves with it; they do not have a profound sense of being a part of this family, the people of God.

How can a competent catechist, a good teacher of faith and religion, convey this to them? It is important that we genuinely love the students with whom we work. What does this do to convey the sense of community? It creates a bond between teacher and the one being taught—and that need not be in a classroom; it can be a parent in a home. That way, when I tell a group of students that they are the Christian community, a family, they realize that I am not just saying something that I have read somewhere, something I want them to memorize. They realize that this statement lives for me as a reality, that I regard the church, the people of God, as my own brothers and sisters to whom I feel bound in friendship and concern. This includes them. In a very literal sense there is a deep bond which unites us.

I may never put this fact into so many words, but as I deal with them, gradually they come to sense that I am genuinely concerned about them and interested in their problems and questions. In this way they come to discover the community of the church and their identity as a part of it. When I do speak to them about the *church,* it begins to take on the basic meaning of "this group of which we are a part."

The second phase of this "church consciousness" which must pervade all our religious formation and religious education is the identification of the young people, genuinely and consistently, with the various patterns within this church. But let us remember that the church is not some vague, material "thing," an organization in an abstract, technical framework. The church is people, and we are those people. Genuine catechesis must create in students a sense of identity with other people, the people who surround them. Otherwise the church is a pure abstraction, and identification with it does nothing to make faith a living reality for them.

How is this taught? We must begin with the very situation of our religious formation. Say, for example, that I am a teacher in a classroom. Somehow I must find the means of letting my students know that we are Christians together. I do not stand apart from them, giving instruction about the church. We share this. We live in common. Moreover, I must lead these young people to identify themselves with one another. From the earliest stages of education we must direct them toward one another. Unless this is achieved, unless they develop concern for and identification with one another, they will never have a deep awareness of the full significance of the Christians assembled in community to celebrate the Eucharist.

In trying to create in all our teaching a sense of identification, then, we start first with a class situation. Next we proceed to the somewhat larger group, the parish. There are many ways of doing this. Perhaps on certain given occasions we can let the children participate in something that the parish is doing. Even though they are small, and even though they can do very little in the Mass situation, we can let them do something. That way, they really sense that they are part of this family and will become interested in the activities of the parish. Even though we know that this may be in the main beyond their understanding, we begin to talk to them about what adults are doing in the parish, some of their projects. Little by little this becomes the context of their thinking, and as they grow into adolescence and adulthood parish participation becomes something familiar to them. It is not an abrupt change from childhood pursuits into the life of the faith. Thus as they come into adulthood and are asked to contribute more to the life of the parish, they will love to do so. Participation has been familiar to them since the time they were little children. Because they have identified themselves with their class, the parish, and the whole church, not just here but throughout the whole world, they feel as though they are a vital part of something important.

We need to teach students that Christianity should be a source of happiness for them. We should tell them about the traditions of their parish and about all the traditions of Christianity over the centuries. This will develop a certain sense of "family pride" in knowing that they are Christians and that all these great achievements of the past, the wonderful accomplishments of Christians, are things with which they can identify themselves. The family of God becomes a context in which their own lives find meaning.

All of this is really part of another major objective in creating a sense of the meaning of "church" for them. We as catechists must present the church as appealing. Unfortunately, many young people grow up being told verbally that the church is wonderful, attractive. But at the same time they absorb—in the home perhaps or in the school, perhaps from their friends or even their teachers—a very subtle impression that there is also much that is burdensome as well. In a way, might it not have been better if we had not been born Catholics and baptized almost immediately? Would it not have been better, perhaps, if allegiance to Christianity were not our obligation? If this is the underlying attitude of parents and teachers, then this is what is conveyed to students no matter what we say verbally. It is important that our own attitude toward Christianity be that it is something greatly attractive, that life is a wonderful thing, and that to be human is marvelous. We must be convinced ourselves that being a Christian is a source of happiness for us. Then only can we teach these young people about Christianity. It is not merely an obligation to complicate young lives. On the contrary, through it children experience happiness and fulfillment. We want our young people to be happy, and because we do we give them this great treasure which is ours, our own faith.

Families get together and share with one another their experiences. The parents tell the children about the things they did when they were young. A certain sense of happiness is created in belonging to this particular family. They do not spend all their lives regretting the fact that somehow they happened to be born into it. So it is with the family of God. It can be a source of happiness and joy. And many of the necessities which are part of the life of Christianity should be presented in this regard.

Perhaps most importantly—and this is a critical point—we should present in this atmosphere of gratitude and happiness the reality of authority within the church. Authority is something which makes it possible for us to have as Christians organized and free lives. You can imagine what Christianity would be like if there were none in the Christian community to order things, to organize, to lead.

Often we get a very inadequate notion of authority. Perhaps sometimes there is an abuse of authority; this happens because we are, after all, human. Though there is an abuse of authority now and then, we have to be careful that we do not adopt a cynical attitude, a consistently negative approach. This will be conveyed almost automatically to the young. We make it so difficult for them to grow up with a balanced view of authority in their own lives as Christians.

The various aspects of our Christian lives must be presented to them in a positive, buoyant, and optimistic fashion. The appeal of the church to young people is one which is related to all their idealisms. We must present the church to them for what it really is, an apostolic community. We are Christians for the sake of others and to make the world a better place for human beings to live and grow in.

Young people take to this. We have seen in recent years the idealism of young people, the interest in movements like the Peace Corps, the way in which they become involved in what demands blood, sweat, and tears. In a sense we deprive them of the very birthright which is theirs as Christians if we do not create an awareness in them that to be a Christian is to be a member of this community faced with a challenge.

As Christians we are called to be apostolic. At the root of this apostolate is more than an interest in projects or a compulsive tendency to keep busy all the time. The foundation of the genuine apostolic mentality of Christianity is love for others, a depth of human concern, a desire to live for others and thereby make our own lives meaningful.

Just mentioning this now and then will accomplish little. It is not a question of telling the students that Christianity is apostolic and then moving on to the next lesson. This is an idea that has to permeate our whole mentality, the whole approach to the teaching of Christianity. Just as in every aspect of our teaching we must be Christ-centered and we must constantly refer to the reality of the present Christ, so in all our teaching we must create for them the sense of the church as a community of faith. We must let them know it for what it is and let them realize that faith is meant to be directed out of itself. Christians should not live in a ghetto and clutch their faith for fear of losing it. They need to be open to humanity, concerned about all the problems of mankind, and dedicated with Christ to doing something about it.

This is the kind of challenge which will make our students sit up and listen to what we are telling them. If they see some reason for learning what it means to be a Christian, they will learn. Few things have more stimulation for students than the notion that they are called as Christians to do something. If we are really going to teach them that the church offers a constant apostolic challenge, I think something further has to be incorporated into our classroom instruction. To some extent this is outside the proper realm of religious education. Instruction is absolutely essential, but what is broader is the creation of a mentality, an attitude, a view of life as a whole and as characteristically Christian.

This broader view of life, this sort of background for all consciousness and activity, must involve the church. If our young people are going to experience deep faith, then we have to give them the opportunity to do something. One discovers what it means to be a Christian by being one. If the church is that sort of vital, dynamic thing, we cannot simply stand before them in a classroom and verbalize. We must start to live Christianity with them, and we must give them opportunities to act. Only in so doing are we presenting the church correctly, providing opportunities for achievement rather than limiting their activity. The church is not something which tells them not to do this and not to do that. It is the context of living, and therefore it offers opportunities far beyond what people would have without it.

There are two contexts to this activity, and both of them influence the lives of our young people. If they are going to develop integrally and completely into Christians, they must have the opportunity to act in apostolate; and they must have the opportunity to act in liturgy. We must give our students a chance to become involved in doing what Christians should be doing. Much depends upon the age level of the group we are teaching and upon the precise social situation in which we find ourselves. It depends upon the concrete needs of the people around us. But with imagination we can provide ways of letting them do things, so that as Christians they discover for themselves the apostolate. Then we can explain to them what it really means to give themselves to people in this way, to visit the sick and to care for them, perhaps to help instruct some of those who do not have good educational opportunities. Only then will they discover how, when they come to liturgy, they are to be a community that acts together.

Our teaching must do more than tell students about the faith. It must give them an opportunity to experience it. If they do, then gathered together as the people and the family of God, they will come to know what it means to be fully and genuinely Christian. They will know that they are related to Christ, not in isolation but in union with their fellow Christians. They will know that they are united with Christ to work with him for the transformation of the world in which men live.

This is what we have seen about faith. It is something which touches the depths of the human being. The Christian accepts Christ in depth and lives with him in order that he and other men may live more fully.

Study outline

The effective teacher of faith must teach within the context of the Christian community, the church

The teacher must create in the students a sense of belonging to this family, the church

How can a competent teacher convey this sense of belonging?
  The teacher must genuinely love the students with whom he works
    He sets up a bond with them, drawing them into the atmosphere of his own identity

As they learn about the church, they sense the reality of their own experience
The teacher must create a sense of shared life in the group
The church is not an organization but a people; we are the church
Unless we Christians have a sense of identification with one another, we will never have community awareness of the celebration of the Eucharist
We must let students sense that they are part of the parish
Their interest and participation in the parish gives them a sense of security
It leads them to identify themselves with the church on a worldwide basis

In the context of community, Christianity becomes a source of happiness for young people

The family of God becomes meaningful to them
We share our treasure of Christianity with them that they may be happy, not that they may be burdened
We should present in this atmosphere of happiness and gratitude the reality of authority within the church
Authority makes it possible for us to have an organized and free life.
A balanced view offsets cynicism
We must present the Church as an apostolic community
Young people respond to the sense of being a member of a community faced with a challenge
We are concerned for others, for the good of the world
Love for others, concern, must permeate our mentality and approach
Christians live in the world, not apart from it
Young people must be given the opportunity to act apostolically
We discover what it means to be a Christian by being one
Opportunities for involvement depend upon age, group, and social circumstances
Faith touches the deepest reaches of the human being. Through it he accepts Christ and lives with him that others may live more fully

Study questions

1 How are the ideas in this talk reflected in the Constitution on the Church?
2 How should these concepts of the Constitution affect a religion program?
3 Evaluate the efforts made thus far in creating a true community in a religion group.
4 What can we do to help young people sense that they are a vital part of a parish?
5 Can an apostolic dimension be built into our religion program?

Further study

Pierre Babin. *Crisis of Faith.* New York: Herder and Herder, 1963.

The Constitution on the Church of Vatican Council II. With a commentary by Gregory Baum, O.S.A. Gleń Rock: Paulist Press, 1965.

Everett J. Morgan, S.J., editor. *The Social Conscience of a Catholic.* Milwaukee: Marquette University Press, 1964.

Brother Savio, C.F.X. "The Religion Class as a Community of the Redeemed," *The Living Light,* Vol. 1 (Fall 1964), 58-63.

Marcel Van Caster, S.J. "The Family, the Parish, Schools, and Groups," *The Structure of Catechetics.* New York: Herder and Herder, 1965. Pp. 215-39.

AP 5'67				
JE 29 '67				
MY 24 '70				
AUG 1 3 1971				